G000048460

THE WELLS OF VISION

This edition published 2002 by SIL Trading Ltd.

ISBN 1 899585 65 6

© Society of the Inner Light 2002

All rights reserved. No reproduction, copy or transmission of
this publication may be made without written permission.
No paragraph of this publication may be reproduced, copied or
transmitted save with written permission or in accordance with
the provision of the Copyright Act 1956 (as amended).
Any person who does any unauthorised act in relation to this
publication may be liable to criminal prosecution and civil
claims for damages.

A CIP catalogue record for this book is available from the
British Library.

Design, Typesetting & Printing by
Clinton Smith Design Consultants, London, NW3 2BD

Printed and bound in Great Britain.

The Society of the Inner Light has no branches nor authorised
representatives and expresses no opinion on other groups.

SIL Trading Ltd is the commercial extension of The Society of the Inner Light -
Registered Charity No; 207213

Its aims and objectives include the propagation of theology and metaphysical religion.

THE WELLS OF VISION

By

Gareth Knight

S.I.L.(Trading) Ltd
38 Steeles Road
London, NW3 4RG

Other books by Gareth Knight

A Practical Guide to Qabalistic Symbolism
Esoteric Training in Everyday Life
Evoking the Goddess (*aka* The Rose Cross and the Goddess)
Experience of the Inner Worlds
Magic and the Western Mind (*aka* A History of White Magic)
Magical Images and the Magical Imagination
Merlin and the Grail Tradition
Occult Exercises and Practices
Tarot and Magic (*aka* The Treasure House of Images)
The Secret Tradition in Arthurian Legend
The Magical World of the Inklings
The Magical World of the Tarot
The Occult: an Introduction
The Practice of Ritual Magic
The Magic of JR Tolkien
The Magical World of C.S Lewis
Pythoness: The Life and Work of Margaret Lumley Brown

Books by Dion Fortune with Gareth Knight

The Magical Battle of Britain
An Introduction to Ritual Magic
The Circuit of Force
Principles of Hermetic Philosophy
Spiritualism and Occultism
Principles of Esoteric Healing

CONTENTS

PREFACE

The chapters in this book consist of articles that appeared in the Inner Light Journal, house journal of the Society of the Inner Light, between Spring 1997 and December 2001. They have as a common theme, aspects of my own magical work and experience.

Awen, the Power in the Magical Cauldron first appeared as a Foreword to the book Awen, the Quest of the Celtic Mysteries by Mike Harris [Sun Chalice, Oceanside, Cal. 1999]

Qabalah and the Occult Tradition was first given as a talk on 30th May 1999 to a conference on Kabbalah and the English Esoteric Tradition, at the Ashmolean Museum, Oxford, organised by the Kabbalah Society.

1
SPEAKING WITH ANGELS

The Sword in the Sun by Anthony Duncan is the record of a remarkable conversation between an angel and a rather surprised Christian priest. A wise and often humorous dialogue that is notable for its insight into several esoteric subjects including the Qabalistic Tree of Life, the inner orders of angels and elementals, reincarnation and the evolution of consciousness.

Above all it is a book about the power of Divine Love - the great unifying energy of the universe - that joins us in brother-hood with angels, elementals and indeed all the living orders under the Creation under the Resurrected and Ascended Christ.

Here is how it began. He was sitting at his desk in the study when he became aware of someone standing beside him, a little behind his left shoulder, saying "We have work to do together. It will not be easy. We must converse in order that others may overhear us and we must speak of deep and weighty matters."

To this the priest replied, "I am fearful - I make no bones about it - I do not relish the thought of being overheard. It will do my standing no good among my fellow clergymen. "What?" they will say, "a clergyman talking to an angel? Haven't the scholars explained angels away? And fancy being overheard! Bad form, that! And who does he want us to think he is?"

And the angel answered, "Does any of this matter? Do I show you the things of God for your own private entertainment? And what nonsense you talk about your brethren. Do they not know you, with all your failings? Are you not projecting upon them your own reaction: jealousy and spiritual pride? And who cares about human scholarship? Do I cease to exist because some clever fellow has abolished me? Let us care for the integrity of the scholar and take his scholarship as we find it."

And the next day the angel came again; but it would be more truthful to say that the clergyman became aware of his presence, for as he well knew, the angel was always present with him. And the angel said: "I am glad you have written that I am always with you, for as you know, I am your Guardian Angel."

To which the priest replied: "I very well remember the occasion when you first showed yourself to me. I was making my thanksgiving after offering the Eucharist, when suddenly, you were there! I saw you with an inner vision; a man-like shape, apparently made of a bright, copper coloured flame. The overwhelming impression I perceived was of an unfathomable love, and directed, of all persons, to me! I fear my description is poor and unflattering."

And the Angel said: "You saw me as I am! The previous day your consciousness was raised in prayer until you found yourself in the presence of many angels and of discarnate human souls. Do you remember both the sense of copper coloured flame and of beings robed in white? The images of heaven in holy scripture have become debased in the minds of mortal men, but their reality is unaffected, as all mortal men shall shortly discover."

This conversation took place in early 1972. I knew Anthony Duncan well at the time. He was the priest who prepared me for confirmation into the Anglican church in 1965, a series of confirmation classes I should say that sparked a great deal of realisation, indeed revelation, on either side. I an initiate of the Mysteries who felt that something was not quite complete in the traditional teaching of the Western Mystery Tradition with its heavy injection of Eastern religious assumptions. He a newly ordained curate in the Church of England, and a natural psychic, who as a regular officer in the British Army had suddenly had the call to resign his commission and become a clergyman.

Two books came out of that series of confirmation classes. My own *Experience of the Inner Worlds* in which I sought to establish a Christ oriented approach to magic without falling into the pitfall of becoming a kind of off beat religious sect. I have since taught a generation of students from it and its practical exercises are based upon a sequence of symbols from another profoundly mystical script from Anthony Duncan called *The Lord of the Dance*.

He for his part, wrote *The Christ, Psychotherapy & Magic*, trying to reconcile all he had learned from me about the Western Mystery Tradition with traditional theology and his vocation as a priest.

Then our ways diverged for a generation until, by some law of cycles and polarities, his books were eventually published by an old student of mine, Mark Whitehead, at Sun Chalice Books, Oceanside, California, who has written a very fine book of his own also using symbols derived from *The Lord of the Dance* entitled *Patterns in Magical Christianity*.

But what are we to make of this business of angels? They seem to be the subject of quite a stir in esoteric circles of late, which, as generally happens with fringe enthusiasms, means plenty of clouds of dense and acrid smoke beyond which one hopes there may be sparks from the heart of a sacred fire.

The principal traditional authority upon angels is *The Celestial Hierarchies*, written under the pseudonym of Dionysius the Areopagite, who had been a friend and associate of St. Paul. It was thus accorded great respect in the medieval church because of its assumed authorship but it was most probably written by a neoplatonist of the 6th century A.D. It was common practice in those days to write anonymously under the name of a famous person as a means of persuading people to read you. Anyhow, under whatever authorship, it remains the traditionally accepted scheme, combining a formal intellectual pattern with some high spiritual insights.

It divides the angelic hosts into a hierarchical scheme of three three-fold orders, nine orders in all. The intention is to demonstrate the translation of divine ideas into events and conditions in the worlds of form.

First Triad: Seraphim, Cherubim, Thrones;

Second Triad: Dominions, Virtues, Powers;

Third Triad: Principalities, Archangels, Angels.

Their specific attributes are appropriate, for the most part, to their names.

Seraphim: These are "burning" or "fiery" ones. Their consuming fire is of super-celestial grace. They are able to look directly into the face of God and live. Thus, as with the traditional lore of eagles, they may fly high and gaze directly upon the Spiritual Sun without being blinded by the excess of glory. As mighty hawks, they may also watch the worlds below from a great height, as the eyes of God. Or, like the eagle of Zeus with Ganymede, they can raise the elect, who may be the cup-bearers of God. A Biblical example of one such would have been Enoch, "who walked with God and was not", and in whose name various Books of Enoch have taught of inner mystical flights. And John, the mystical evangelist, has as his emblem the eagle.

Cherubim: Their name means "fullness of knowledge". They are thus mediators of divine wisdom, of the transcendental light. As spirits of illumination they may be conceived as great beacon lights, or celestial flambeaux. In this they are like the stars themselves, their light may form patterns or celestial runes of wisdom, like paradisal constellations; revelations of the seven-fold light.

Thrones: Literally their name means "seats" but they are perhaps best regarded as "chariots of fire", like that which took Elijah to glory. In this they may be regarded as similar to the Auphanim, or "Wheels" of the Throne of God of mystical Hebraic tradition, revolving discs of glory. In this triad of celestial powers we have those closest to the Godhead itself. Firebirds (as eagles or phoenixes); Beacons (or torches or sanctuary lamps or light houses); Fiery Chariots (each a "siege perilous"). All are closely aligned with light and fire as far as our limited human consciousness goes. These are tremendous powers that the individual human soul would find overwhelming, unless fully indwelt and protected by divine grace. For the light and the fire and the intense movement would burn up all dross, or what, in currently unfashionable terms, could be called "sin". In a reincarnationary context this might be seen as an instant resolution of all karma - a self immolating act in its intensity and suddenness - unrelieved by being spread out in time.

Dominions: These impart, and are custodians of, the principles of order and justice. They are the upholders of codes of behaviour and moral responsibilities. That is, all natural law, whether expressed through the natural instincts of the animal creation, (parental care, filial devotion, and the like), or the high aspirations of the righting of wrongs or alleviation of sufferings on a wider scale.

Virtues: Traditionally these are bestowers of grace and valour, which gives expression to spiritual integrity. This can be personal, or in service to a cause, or loyalty to a body of principles. They seek to put into effect the moral principles formulated by the Dominions.

Powers: These give providential aid to the physical expression of the principles upheld by the other angelic orders of this triad. They are controllers of circumstance, the cause of coincidence and synchronicities. They ensure that the right soul is in the right place at the right time. On the wider world scene this may be an Alexander or a Charlemagne or a Churchill, but there is a whole host of lesser events which they may control.

Thus in the second tried we have the level of moral principles, of law givers and law makers and law upholders. Each in their way provides a mix of the moral functions that are to become the basis of expressions of human civilisation.

Principalities: These might be called angelic princes. They are said by Dionysius to exhibit divine lordship and true service. In this they may be equated with the folk souls or group angels of races and nations. The same order of angels in lesser degree influence the esprit de corps of human organisations and associations, the spirit of neighbourhood or of the family or any other coherent human grouping. In their more transitory form they may indwell audiences or crowds, and in broader action in the history of civilisations and nations or popular movements.

Archangels: Archangels, and angels too, are generic titles commonly used to indicate any of the celestial hierarchies, but in Dionysius they are more specifically assigned titles. Archangels he sees as imprinting upon all things the "Divine Seal", whereby the universe is the written word of God. In them we may therefore see the more detailed principles of patterning, not only that which goes to make up the atomic structure of the physical elements but also the systems of life organisms. They are thus intimately connected with the means of expression for the Lords of Flame, Form and Mind, as also of Humanity or Civilisation.

Angels: These "minister to all men and to the things of nature" according to Dionysius, and so have a more individual association with man, higher animals, and the creatures of the elements. We also have the conception of the Holy Guardian Angel which is sometimes associated with or confused with the personal Higher Self. This is an understandable area of confusion because the angel will be seeking to help the individual to open up to the intimations of higher consciousness, which may not at first be readily distinguishable from the voice of promptings of the angel itself.

So much for the Dionysian system, which, it should be said, is not the only one. Variations exist from various medieval authorities, and also in the Hebraic tradition of the Qabalah,

15

but generally speaking a triadic system holds good for practical purposes of elementary understanding. And no human understanding of angels is anything beyond the elementary. Angelology suffers from a paucity of information, as invisible helpers are, by definition, invisible! The more effective their work, the less they are likely to be noticed. The divine, and the demonic, share each in their way, particularly in modern times, the experience of their works being taken for granted and themselves not to exist. This condition, according to *The Screwtape Letters* of C. S. Lewis, is one of the evil angels' great modern achievements!

So while we have on the one hand the very broad generalisations of the nine orders of the system of Dionysius, we must also remember that the participation of angels in the created order extends throughout every part of it, from atomic nucleus to galactic super-cluster, with many ranges of intelligent life expression in between, not only upon the outer levels but upon the inner dimensions as well.

Despite our intellectual limitations, (and to a large extent because of them), it can help to simplify and systematise, as long as we do not assume that the glittering glorious reality is quite so cut and dried and accounted for as our simple charts. The mighty choirs of the heavenly host are not a kind of transcendental civil service. This needs to be borne in mind particularly when comparing one man made system of angelic orders with another, say the Dionysian with the Qabalistic.

We might well take a leaf from Dante's book, where in Canto xxix of the *Paradiso* he says of the angels that their nature ranks so wide that neither mortal speech nor thought can conceive their full extent. And he compares their nature to myriads of tiny mirrors, each reflecting the will of God.

Thus there is no conflict between the concept of the unity of the one God, and the untold millions of angels who reflect and express the divine will.

For an example of how angelic powers might impinge directly upon the human condition we could turn to the novel *The Place of the Lion* by Charles Williams. Fiction is able to present truths that cannot be accepted as fact by prevailing intellectual fashion. Williams' novel is based firmly upon the Platonic tradition that there is a world of divine ideas or archetypes behind the outer world we know with our physical senses.

These figure as animal images, which from tribal totems to Aesop's fables and extending to the signs of the zodiac, have ever served to represent particular modes of consciousness: the swiftness of the horse, the purity of the unicorn, the patience of the tortoise. And central to the theme of Williams' book is the fierceness of the lion, the subtlety of the serpent, the beauty of the butterfly. These are not mere intellectual conceits but principles of activity and divine expression in action, for which these animal forms serve as tuning devices in consciousness, or "magical images".

A critical point in the novel depends upon the significance of Adam having "named" all the animals. This is not seen as a primitive attempt at the classification of fauna. The animals referred to are not zoological species but Platonic ideas, or forms of divine expression, by means of which early man built up a personality and system of self consciousness. The "naming" of the powers, is humanity's gaining control over the archetypes within the dawning individualised psyche, rather than being immersed within a sea of animal-like forms of group consciousness in some form of 'participation mystique'.

The process may be seen at a further stage of Biblical development in the story of Noah and the ark. Here the process is one of taking the archetypal powers on board in balanced pairs of function. The ark, as representation of human individualised consciousness, was developed to precise measurements by divine instruction. All previous humanoid forms of expression have been superseded, (by a flood of undifferentiated consciousness overwhelming them), and we have a new phase of human expression. This is the potential of the ego oriented man, in the ark of his own self consciousness, no longer swamped by free ranging uncontrolled 'animal' forces, or what we have come to call, in one of its aspects at any rate, the collective unconscious.

The critical importance of this stage of human development is emphasised by it being regarded as the 'first covenant' between God and man, and its image is the rainbow. This again is no primitive attempt to explain meteorological phenomena. It represents a profoundly optimistic teaching of the heavenly bow of aspiration that directs the arrow of human potential to the spiritual heights. There is a correlating resonance with the bow and arrow, one of the first technological expressions of man's conquest of nature. This combined with the ability to hunt at a distance with the utilisation of dynamic physical principles in the elasticity and potential energy of muscle power transmitted to and stored in taut wood and thong. And the wood of the bow, the gut of the bow string, and feathered flight, wooden shaft, and flint or metal of the arrow head, are a magical demonstration of man's potential dominance of the natural world.

Mankind enters the scene as the next spiritual hierarchy. The Lords of Civilisation, or Humanity, succeed to the experimentation and rule of the Lords of Mind, and before them, of the Lords of Form and Flame.

There are, however, other celestial beings whose influence rays upon the Earth and upon mankind, here and now. It is a matter of spiritual evolution as to how we interact with them or are responsive to them. This has traditionally been expressed in the pictorial imagery of star lore.

At the other end of the cosmic scale are the building blocks of the universe, which are shown in the patterns of the structure of the elements on the physical plane. The physical plane is the "Ring Pass Not" of the cosmos. We cannot "go through" matter to another level of denser reality.

Any possibility of some kind of super-density takes us into the mathematical concept of a "black hole", from which nothing can escape, not even light itself. This is currently a favoured speculation of scientific cosmology although metaphysicians may well doubt whether light itself can be subjected to such confinement as is thought possible by those who consider it no more than a form of electromagnetic phenomena.

The concept has a certain horrifying fascination. It depicts a kind of cosmic equivalent of a quicksand or whirlpool, or the psychological parallels of obsession or psychosis. A vortex that exists for its own sake, that takes and apparently never gives, a negation of all spiritual values.

However, the concept of an interacting vortex, capable of polarised relationship with other vortices, is one that is fundamental to the general metaphysical theory of creative principles.

All manifestation is based upon the union of opposites, in complementary polarity, and the appropriate image for this is a vortex. This applies to the human personality as well as to great beings of the inner worlds, be they Star Lords or angels, or the lesser builders who inform the atoms of physical nature. The whole tenor of Dion Fortune's *The Cosmic Doctrine* is an evolutionary development in spiritual terms of a system of vortices. And in the vision of the Protestant mystic Jacob Boehme the vortex is an image at the very fount of creation itself. It is the highest mystery of the Godhead.

There are, according to Boehme's revelation, myriads of angelic worlds beyond that of the human. Nonetheless there are angelic beings within the human realm of consciousness who perform various acts of intercession and control as agents of the Divine Will.

This can vary from the patterning of the building blocks of the universe we know, from atoms to life organisms, and the overseeing of the elemental consciousness involved in the function of biological mechanisms. And at a higher level, in the broad categories outlined by Dionysius in *The Celestial Hierarchies,* interceding in the complex pattern of human culture from the history of civilisations to the guidance of individuals.

Boehme believed implicitly that God, absolute and self created, and in eternity, desired to reveal Himself to mankind, but that this revelation required intermediaries who were distinct from Himself, and a mirror of Himself, the mightiest of whom have been called 'the Seven Spirits before the Throne'.

It is perhaps significant that the simple shoe-maker Boehme was given these revelations at a time when the materialist cloud was about to obscure the spiritual heavens in the West. His life, from 1575 to 1624, coincides with the stirrings of the scientific method. He was the first of an important trio, the others being Swedenborg and Blake, who kept the consciousness of the angelic realms alive during the dark days.

And in a litany recited by the angel in *The Sword in the Sun* is an evocation of the creation and establishment of the world, taking in the metaphysical dimension, that has resonances with the spheres of the Tree of Life.

> The Father, introspective, sees Himself, the Son,
> Standing upon his mental stage.
> The Son will have some fellow-players,
> And, out of Love, brings them to life.
> First, the Archangels to construct the stage
> With Angels helping.
> Then comes Man,
> Stage manager.
> The cast: a Pan
> For every world the angels make;
> And Elemental beings everywhere;
> Spirits of rock, and field, and hill,
> Devas of plants and elements;
> And all constructed, all alive,
> Formed firm by Him who made them, of his Love.

2
SIR WALTER RALEGH
AND THE PRINCESS POCAHONTAS

There might well be a discipline known as esoteric history, which is to say, elements of history that are redolent with "magical images" of personalities who embodied principles or archetypes that are important either to the nation, or to the world at large.

For those of us who are concerned with the dynamics of group souls these personalities can be the focus of very rewarding meditational and visualisation work, in what might be called the macro-psychotherapy of the collective unconscious if we were looking for a high sounding name for it. These historical characters invariably have a powerful presence in the imagination through legendary stories of one kind or another, and often this presence is so powerful that it can be exploited commercially as a vehicle for mass entertainment. Thus figures such as Richard the Lionheart or Mary Queen of Scots feature ever and again in film and historical novel.

A recent addition to this band of celebrities to have achieved cinematic stardom, courtesy of Walt Disney, is one who has been of prime interest to me over a number of years, the Princess Pocahontas of Virginia. Pocahontas is one of those important bridging figures between nations and cultures, and her story is part of that very rich period in our national development when Elizabethan seamen traversed the great waters of the world.

The motive of most of these old sea dogs was seeking treasure, by trade or exploration and some deeds of derring-do upon the Spanish Main. One of them, however, Sir Walter Ralegh, had a more constructive aim. He sought to establish settlements, particularly in the New World, to develop agriculture, manufacturing and trade. In this he had as mentor and source of inspiration, the Elizabethan magus, mathematician and geographer, Dr. John Dee, whose navigational charts provided guidance for the adventuring seafarers, and who first conceived the idea of overseas dominions in a "new Atlantis". Ralegh spent a large part of his fortune and the best efforts of his life to carry into effect this great dream, which he dedicated to Queen Elizabeth, "Astraea", the Star Virgin and destined Empress of the Britons of the New World.

Scholar and poet as well as man of action and leader of men, Ralegh touched the heart of the queen with his courtly and extravagant affection, and she heaped honour and fortune upon him, at least until the time of his marriage.

Dr. John Dee in his capacity of historian had spent a lot of time seeking justification for a British presence in the New World, in defiance of the Pope's decree that all should be divided between Spain and Portugal. In the capacity of entrepreneur, along with Adrian and Humphrey Gilbert, he sought to explore the Canadian seaboard in search of a North-west passage to the Indies and Cathay, a quest that eventually cost Humphrey his life, although he and John Dee came within a whisker of owning half of Canada between them.

Sir Humphrey happened also to be the half brother of Sir Walter Ralegh, and it was him he chose as a man he could trust to lead the enterprise of founding a new colony. The queen would not allow her favourite and Master of the Horse to embark on such long and perilous journeys away from her. However, she granted a mandate for their company to seek new lands and claim them for the Crown, a process confirmed by the simple ancient ceremony of cutting a sod and taking a hazel wand.

The first attempts were fraught with danger and disaster but at length the first English colony was established, in 1585, which in honour of the Queen, and at her suggestion, was named Virginia. The first two settlements failed to establish themselves in a hostile environment and it was not for another 21 years that a third attempt was successful, by which time Ralegh was a prisoner in the Tower of London under James I. When the Virginia Company made landfall in Chesapeake Bay they built a triangular fort with palisades which they called Jamestown, on the James River, named after the new Stuart king.

A leading spirit in this adventure of 1606 was Captain John Smith, a soldier of fortune who had all the daring and resourcefulness characteristic of the old Elizabethan seamen. When he fell prisoner of local tribesmen he preserved his life for many months by the display of seemingly magical powers and astute exploitation of his superior technical knowledge. Eventually he was taken before Powhattan, the chief of all the Indians of the area, to decide whether he was to live or die.

The English adventurer found himself standing before the Indian chief, surrounded by warriors, amongst whom was a young girl, the daughter of the chief. The Indian braves talked animatedly between themselves, apparently relating the story of his capture, his powers as a medicine man, and debating his fate. In the end two flat stones are placed on the ground and as Smith was spread-eagled upon them two young warriors with heavy clubs stepped forward showing every intention of doing him to death.

At this moment the chief's young daughter sprang forward with a cry and flung her arms about John Smith, placing herself between the prisoner and the clubs. This action was met by great excitement among the Indians and after long palaver they conveyed to him that he was reprieved. They had a great feast and thereafter he was treated with great ceremony and respect.

His story became famous, as to how he owed his escape to Pocahontas, who had saved his life by claiming him as a husband. Smith, and most other Europeans who heard the story, thought it a thrilling tale of romantic love, but there are others who see in it a ritual initiation into the tribe through a symbolic death and resurrection, with the chief's daughter as his mystical sponsor. If this is the case, then a union was effected between two cultures and two continents by means of a mystery ritual.

Pocahontas was ever afterwards described by Smith as an interceding angel, not only in this dramatic event, but on several later occasions. When he had returned to the fort of Jamestown she often used to visit, bringing supplies of food, which helped to stave off the starvation that constantly threatened the small community. She also gave warning of possible attacks or acts of treachery by native malcontents whenever they were threatened.

John Smith was later elected President of the Jamestown Council after being badly injured by an explosion of gunpowder, when his tobacco pipe accidentally ignited a powder horn. He was put on ship for home, and it was widely believed that he had died. Pocahontas, then aged sixteen, married an Indian, Korouim, of whom nothing is known but who seems to have died or disappeared within the next three years.

By this time, another Captain, Samuel Argall, brought reinforcements from England and went exploring for food among Indians on the river Potomac. Hearing that Pocahontas was visiting these tribes, he used a friendly Indian chief and his wife to persuade Pocahontas to board his ship, whereupon he took her prisoner and held her to ransom in exchange for eight Englishmen who were being held by her now disaffected father.

Realising that she had been betrayed Pocahontas nonetheless showed such great natural dignity that she was treated as an honoured guest. She came to assume the role of one who could bring back faith and friendship between her father and the English, a mediatrix between the colony of strangers and her people.

During this time she began to receive instruction in the Christian faith and was baptised, taking the Christian name of Rebecca. Peace was established and confirmed by her marriage to John Rolfe, an Englishman from Norfolk, whose agricultural endeavours in raising tobacco commercially later preserved the colony by putting its economy on a firm footing.

Seven years had passed since the English had re-settled the Virginia territory and the Indians realised that their local chief had decided to ally his people to them by the marriage of his daughter. A time of friendly commerce commenced, John Rolfe became Secretary and Recorder of the colony, and Pocahontas bore him a child whom they named Thomas.

Two years later a visit was arranged to England. They landed first at Plymouth and John Smith then wrote to the queen of James I, Anne of Denmark, commending Pocahontas to her, as "the first Christian ever of that nation, the first Virginian who ever spoke English or had a child in marriage by an Englishman." The Virginia Company supported her and her son at a well known inn off Fleet Street, at the sign of the Bell that, tradition says, was later known as La Belle Sauvage because of her stay.

Later, for fresher air, she moved to Brentford, near Syon House. She was presented at court to the King and Queen, attended a court masque for the Twelfth Night celebrations of 1617, and visited her husband John Rolfe's family home at Heacham Hall in Norfolk.

On her return to London she had meetings of a different sort, arranged by George Percy, an early member of the Virginia Company who as a founder of Jamestown had avoided the ignominy of his family's suspected involvement in the Gunpowder Plot. He took her to the Tower of London to see his brother, the Earl of Northumberland, who was known as the Wizard Earl because of his alchemical interests. With the Earl was another distinguished prisoner, the first begetter of the Virginia venture, Sir Walter Ralegh, with his high forehead, dark eyes, iron grey hair and beard, and splendidly dressed in the now rather old fashioned Elizabethan style.

It must have been a strange experience for the Indian princess, being conducted by the constable of the Tower past the lions and ravens kept within it, through dark and damp corridors where the air was cold and heavy with the smell of mildew, until she and George Percy were ushered into the Earl's chamber, where he was kept in a manner befitting his means and his rank. A roaring fire burning in the chimney, a candelabrum ablaze with candles, and a strong smell of incense and cloves, whilst in an adjoining room might be seen an alchemical still and retorts.

The young Indian maiden was announced as Princess Pocahontas, daughter of the Emperor of Virginia, and as a memento of the memorable visit the old Earl gave her a pair of ear rings, made of ovals of mother of pearl set in twists of silver.

We might even imagine the spirit of Dr. John Dee present at this scene, who had died nine years before, but whose early vision and wisdom had brought these people together.

Early in 1617 Samuel Argall, while still in England, was elected Deputy Governor of Virginia and planned to return, accompanied by John Rolfe and Pocahontas. Together with her young son Thomas they embarked on Argall's ship "The George", and sailed down river from London just before the Spring equinox.

The last place for ships to take on fresh water and food in those days was Gravesend, a huddle of houses round a tall church and a three storied inn, twenty-five miles down river from London. Here, where many illustrious visitors first set foot on English soil, was to be the last resting place of Pocahontas.

She was taken ill, probably by a variety of the common cold, and when their ship dropped anchor, she was carried onto the little wharf and the hundred yards or so to the great inn. A doctor was summoned but it was too late, and here in the early Spring of 1617 she died.

The funeral took place in the parish church of St George and her remains were placed in the chancel, the place reserved for clergy and notable parishioners. Then the ship resumed its journey, but her little son Thomas was put off the ship at Plymouth. He later played a prominent part in the affairs of the colony of Virginia, and in recent times a female descendent became the wife of Woodrow Wilson, President of the United States and founder of the League of Nations.

There now stands in the churchyard of St George's, Gravesend, a statue of Pocahontas, the replica of an original that stands in Jamestown, Virginia. The churchyard is laid out with grass and flowers and is known as Princess Pocahontas Garden. The church keeps replicas of the chalice and paten used by the settlers of 1607, which were presented to the present Queen Elizabeth on her visit to Virginia on the 350th anniversary of the landing.

Within the east end of the church are stained glass windows celebrating Pocahontas - "the non-pareil of Virginia." These were unveiled by the United States ambassador in 1914 as a gift of the Virginia Chapter of the American Society of Colonial Dames. One shows the story of Rebecca, the Christian name she took. The other that of Ruth - a similar story to her own of brave love and unshaken truthfulness by one who, though not of the chosen race of Israel, was an ancestor of King David.

There is also a stained glass portrait of Pocahontas, a moving image of her in Jacobean courtly dress, with high hat and starched ruff, holding an ostrich feather fan, and wearing the ear rings given her by the Wizard Earl in the presence of Sir Walter Ralegh.

Places to see: It is never a waste of time to visit places associated with archetypal historical characters of this type, some kind of etheric contact seems to be ever alive, so the following may be of interest to visit:

St. George's church, Gravesend with its stained glass windows and statue of Pocahontas in Princess Pocahontas Gardens. This church, which was threatened with demolition in 1951 is preserved as a Chapel of Unity by the Church Commissioners under a trust fund, dedicated as a symbolic point of contact between the old world and the new.

Heacham Hall, Norfolk, family seat of the Rolfe family. Not open to the public but the area worth a visit just for its lavender farming.

A statue of John Smith stands in the churchyard of *St Mary le Bow, Cheapside* - while his remains lie not far away in *St Sepulchre's church, Newgate,* which also contains a replica of the Holy Sepulchre at Jerusalem.

Sherborne, the family seat of Sir Walter Ralegh, should certainly not be missed. It was afterwards bought by the Digby family, whose Sir Kenelm Digby was a keen alchemist. Afficionados of Dion Fortune will be fascinated to see **DEO NON FORTUNAS** appearing all over hall and town, the family motto of the Digby family.

Nearby is *Cerne Abbas,* site of the famous giant, and where Sir Walter on account of his activities with the so-called "School of Night" was brought before the magistrates accused of witchcraft. Here are also the remains of an old abbey, where Christian and pagan forces seem to have achieved a remarkable and peaceful equilibrium. Whilst beyond the bottom of the churchyard and its 17th century graves, is a grove of lime trees hiding a holy well, dedicated to St Catherine.

Syon Hall the seat of the Wizard Earl, near Brentford, on the river Thames, and much further down river, the Tower of London where he experimented in alchemy and Ralegh wrote his "History of the World" and where sailors used to cheer him as they sailed past, somewhat to the annoyance of the king.

In the *Ashmolean Museum, Oxford,* Powhattan's robe is displayed. There is also a replica of it in *St Mary's church, Lambeth,* which is now a botanical museum, and where Captain Bligh's remains rest. The "Bounty" was employed on horticultural duties at the time of the famous mutiny. Another interesting titbit about this church is the stained glass window that looks remarkably like the Fool of the Tarot.

Although no old building stands there now, there is a little square of green with a bench seat just by where Dr John Dee lived at *Mortlake,* on the other side of the road from the church, and with access to the river strand which must be very much the same as Dr Dee knew it, and remains an evocative site because of this.

Books to read:
Two books on Pocahontas, out of print unless the Disney film has renewed some publisher's interest, but quite readily available on the second hand market, are *Pocahontas and her World* by Philip L. Barbour [Robert Hale 1969] and a novel *Pocahontas,* or *the Nonpareil of Virginia* by David Garnett [Chatto & Windus 1933]. Notable biographies of Sir Walter Ralegh include *Sir Walter Raleigh* by Milton Waldman [Collins 1928 & 1943], *That Great Lucifer* by Margaret Irwin

[Chatto & Windus 1960], *A Play of Passion* by Stephen Coote [Macmillan 1993], and *The Creature in the Map* by Charles Nicholl [Vintage 1996]. Of Dr John Dee *John Dee 1527-1608* by Charlotte Fell Smith [Constable 1909], *John Dee: Scientist, Geographer, Astrologer & Secret Agent to Elizabeth I* by Richard Deacon [Robert Muller 1968], *John Dee: the World of an Elizabethan Magus* by Peter J. French [Routledge & Kegan Paul 1972] and *The Queen's Conjuror, the Science and Magic of Dr Dee* by Benjamin Wooley [Harper Collins 2001]. Biographies of close associates include *The Traces of Thomas Hariot* by Muriel Rukeyser [Victor Gollancz 1972] and *The Life of Sir Humphrey Gilbert* by William Gilbert Gosling [Constable 1911 & Greenwood Press 1970].

3
THE WELLS OF VISION

In the Western Esoteric Tradition we tend to associate practical work with formal assemblies, often in a corporate meeting place elaborately furnished with symbols. However this does not always have to be the situation and some very effective work can be done when just two or three are gathered together in a normal domestic setting.

As in individual meditation it is helpful to set aside a regular period perhaps on a weekly rather than a daily basis. Whatever the time interval, a regular meeting seems to set up a kind of track in space that has some effect on one's own body clock. It may also prove helpful to any contact we may have on the inner planes, where they may not have the advantage of a handy clock on the mantle-piece but can more easily judge the passage of linear time from the pulse of a regular interval between meetings.

Here follow some notes taken over a period of six weeks in the Spring of 1985 where just such an arrangement was worked by two of us on a Sunday evening. The interesting thing about this particular set of meetings is that they form a little vignette of picking up a contact, identifying the communicator, and receiving some specific practical teaching, in general and particular terms, after which the communicator took his leave as unexpectedly as he came.

The matter of identity makes an interesting little case study in itself, for it raises questions that are relevant to the identity of any inner plane communicator of esoteric teachings. There is always the question as to whether the identity claimed or revealed is an actual or a symbolic one. In practical terms this is a somewhat academic point for the crux of the matter is the quality of communication rather than any claims as to its origination. The oft-quoted remarks from such a source in the introduction to *The Cosmic Doctrine* apply in all such cases, whether or not the communicator is of the rank of a master. "The Masters as you picture them are all 'imagination' . Note well that I did not say the Masters were imagination: I said 'The Masters as you picture them.' What we are you cannot realise and it is a waste of time to try to do so, but you can imagine us on the astral plane and we can contact you through your imagination, and although your mental picture is not real or actual, the results of it are real and actual."

The technique that we used for these particular sessions was precisely that of building pictures in the imagination, conjoined with the faculty of letting spontaneous images also rise. There was no question of being in any kind of trance or semi-hypnotic state. The two of us simply sat face to face, and jointly described and visualised what appeared to the inner eye and ear. Some novelists, including Dion Fortune, claim to write their works in just such a fashion, so the whole process is more like jointly writing a book rather than indulging in any weird practice of raising spooks. The only difference from creative writing is one of spiritual intention, we were seeking as an end result instruction for ourselves rather than entertainment of others.

Our usual contact did not put in an appearance, and we sat there in a slight quandary until R. picked up a raven flying over a whirlpool in the sea. The raven descended and seemed somehow to take up a "thread" of water up from this vortex and began to construct a castle in the air from it. This soon achieved some size and solidity to the point when we felt impelled to pass over a causeway that led into the castle.

Here we found a large open hall which was something like a great set of film studios, with booths all round the place, each one containing an historical scene. We found that if we went up to any one of these scenes it would set it in motion and we would find ourselves within it as part of the scene, rather like being in a vivid "path working".

However, we did not get deeply involved in any of these attractions for at the end of the hall and drawing our attention in some subtle way was a man in a twentieth century pin-striped suit. He seemed very pleased and indeed proud of all that was going on around us and described it as an "interesting device". He had a moustache and smoked a pipe, and there was a strong image of him tamping down the tobacco, and afterwards putting it into his pocket.

He seemed to be a literary figure and our assumption was that he represented one of the "Lords of Story". That is to say one of a group of writers of the late Victorian and Edwardian era who had, without necessarily having any overt esoteric interests, by some of their writings, introduced magical or other mind stretching dynamics into the group soul. The group seemed to include writers like Rudyard Kipling, Edith Nesbit, James Barry, H. G. Wells and narrative poets such as John Masefield and Alfred Noyes.

Our attention had first been drawn to this group at the end of a very powerful public workshop some time previously, when in a spontaneous visualised journey they seemed to be associated in some way with the constellation Draco, that coils around the Pole Star.

Be this as it may, following upon this home-spun working I looked up a number of photographs of literary figures, comparing them to the figure seen in our vision, and thought that the nearest likeness might be either Masefield or Wells. On the strength of this in a secondhand bookshop the following Saturday I picked up and purchased a book by H.G.Wells, which had the somewhat evocative title of *The Shape of Things to Come,* and when I began to read it I found to my surprise that the Introduction was called The Dream Book of Dr. Raven..

As the vision of the previous Sunday leading to the contact with the pipe smoking gentleman had commenced with a raven, was this a clue confirming identity? Bearing in mind that the castle contained moving vignettes of scenes from history, one was also struck by the fact that H.G.Wells had been famous for writing a history of the world entitled *An Outline of History.*

7.30 p.m. Sunday 17th March 1985

We had been, I have to confess, rather preoccupied with other affairs immediately prior to this session, and indeed might well have missed it had not an inner voice come into the imagination of R. as she stood over the ironing board, saying "Set up a session".

Having done so, the same contact as last week came through and did indeed seem to take on the physiognomy and personality of Wells. He started to talk about time and said that time was of great interest to him, but although he had been much interested in the past his greater concern was with the future, and the flow of the future. He seemed to want to impress us with the idea that rather than seeking to reconstruct the mysteries of the past it was very important to try to reconstruct in the here and now the ideas for the mysteries of the future. In other words that one can influence the future by magical means by building the seeds of the future in the present.

"How many people learn from the lessons of the past?" he insisted, "Would we not be better occupied in laying down the pattern for the future?"

It later occurred to me that this communication was very much in the Utopian tradition - which has antecedents in Plato in his Socratic dialogues, in Sir Thomas More who actually wrote the book from which Utopia derives its name, and Renaissance magical figures such as Thomasso Campanella who tried to interest the Pope of the day in the pattern for an ideal City of the Sun based upon the pattern of celestial archetypes, and so on. Wells of course had not only written a history of the world but had first come to popular fame by his science fiction novels of the future, including *The Time Machine*. More specifically *The Shape of Things to Come* is the record of a deceased (fictional) League of Nations official, Dr. Raven, who had achieved the facility of dreaming in the future and his dream book is a history of the future of the world until well into the 21st century.

The contact on this occasion seemed to crystallise very much into the personality of Wells, even though it was not our aim in any of this to forge a kind of spiritualist contact with the personality of the deceased writer. Our focus of interest was upon the message not the medium for it. But the contact did indeed seem a close and personal one to the point of him noting that R. had not read his book, which seemed to afford him a little difficulty in getting some concepts through.

7.30 p.m. Sunday 24th March, 1985

We had, during the earlier part of this weekend attended a group meeting in the west country. There we had spoken of these two "Wells contacts" to others in the group. At the time we did this R. had a strong feeling of Wells being present, as if sitting on the settee beside her. We did not particularly feel like having another esoteric session when we got home as we were feeling tired, however HGW (as we might as well now call him) insisted on coming through. He said he had been with us at the meeting and also in on our discussion in the car coming home, and had been much interested.

He was impressed with what he called our "technology of the mind" in the form of ritual, and said there were others working on these lines too. One got the impression that he rather regretted not having interested himself in these matters during his physical life time. He was of course always something of a sceptical agnostic.

In answer to a question discussed previously in the day as to what his "esoteric status" might be, he said that some who were interested enough in the fate of humanity on Earth were allowed, or enabled, to make and maintain contact in this way. He was not a particularly religious man but was impressed by our techniques. He explained that he used the image of himself puffing a pipe to maintain our concentration, and said it did not taste of tobacco.

The New Jerusalem, he said, was an important image, and of particular import in what we had been discussing was the importance of "humanity" over "the system." That the most obscene word in current usage was the term "mega-death" (at that time bandied about quite a lot in discussions on the politics of nuclear deterrence in the Cold War). Yet the scientist who is using these concepts is concerned with the protection or preservation of his own vision of Utopia or the way to it. It was thus important that we should build our own vision of Utopia and not leave it to others.

He also wanted us to think about how the past affects the present, and the present the future, in terms of psychological problems and all that stem from them. "Does the phoenix carry the memory of its previous existence?" was a striking phrase he used, in conjunction with the concept that if we could cut off the influence of the past we would we be freer to build a better present and future.

8.50 p.m. Sunday 31st March 1985

(The later time of this and subsequent meetings is a consequence of moving to British Summer Time).

There was considerable difficulty in picking up the contact at first because we had just returned (late) from the Prediction Festival and were "hedged about", as he put it, by thought forms. Under instruction from him, to facilitate contact we visualised them as being two-dimensional, like playing cards, and then flattened them.

It is noticeable that he does not let us read his mind, or take imaginative pictures directly from him, but insists on talking - so communication with him is a question of picking up words.

One of the great mistakes he said that he and other builders of Utopias had made was to construct them in some far off place or time or condition. They should be constructed as being in the here and now on Earth.

He referred to the Draco figures, what we had previously referred to as "Lords of Story" as "the Chroniclers". He stressed the importance of writing. Writing was important because it had an element of permanence and could be re-activated by those who read it. Magical work, "in the ether" as he called it, was less lasting but was more immediately powerful.

He said many energies were being channelled into the planet at the present time, (that is to say over the past few years and in the immediate future years), to help towards the building of a perfect Earth.

At the end he re-activated the Prediction Festival thought forms and mixed in as a person within the crowd of them. He said that they all represented different streams and energies coming in but that all had a common aim, to build a better Earth. He asked us to join hands with the two nearest us, and then all to join in the linking up in a great chain of all who had attended the Festival. From this a light grew which spread out all over the town and surrounding area.

He asked if we had read *The Wonderful Visit,* a book he had written about angels visiting and walking the Earth.

At the end R said that she felt that there was a two way flow in these contacts with him, that he was probably learning from us at the same time that we were learning from him. This, I suppose, is a natural exchange of energies and polarity flow.

8.30 p.m. Sunday 7th April 1985

HGW talked about time, and the difficulties of seeing the wood for the trees, or the tree for the leaves, or the leaf for the veins within it, and the need to get an overview. "Time is movement." he said.

He gave us an interesting experiment to try. We had to imagine we were each looking through the tube of a microscope at ourselves. Then we had to, as it were, increase the magnification of the microscope, so as to become conscious of seeing ourselves as part of a group, then as part of a nation, then of a continent, then of a planet. As one does this, so in effect one's point of vision at the eyepiece is being pushed further out into space, and the tube of the microscope is gradually lengthening, and consciousness is moving gradually from that of the personality to that of the spirit. This brings about ancillary sensations. At first of being buffeted by winds and then trying to see through obscuring clouds, which obscure the eye of the spirit from seeing its individual being on earth, but the aim is to clear this view.

Then became aware of other planets and heavenly bodies in space, with the knowledge that this was the level of dreams and aspirations, where we can dream and see clearly, and the spirit is free of the limitations of space and time. After this, began to become aware of angels all about the planet, mediating down lines of light to it, and had the realisation that we need to try to maintain or to recover awareness of these beings, and also to try to be aware of ourselves as "spirits on Earth".

The exercise concludes with going back down in vision via the microscope through the various levels, of cloud, wind, stages of group awareness, to the individual centred with attention on his or her own physical space.

At the end of this session HGW took time to speak to me personally. He walked along a Greek looking path before me and his gait was similar to what is described of Socrates - in fact he almost seemed to turn into this figure. Then I was standing with him and Socrates together. There was an impression that we had all been close together in the flesh in ancient days, and were thus able to work closely together now. We were all three, for a moment, suddenly standing outside of the planet, in space. Then we were back again. A crystal form of a particular shape and colour appeared as a linking symbol between us. There was a tremendous power in this. My crown chakra was very evident like a sensation of pins and needles over the cranium. R. could only see a very bright white light in all of this, and we both had some difficulty getting down into normal consciousness again.

8.30 p.m. Sunday 14th April 1985

HGW appeared, but more as a fellow sitter than a communicator, as we all watched the images rise. Many images came, particularly feminine ones, and it seemed like a résumé of the past few years' of work with the feminine principle.

It culminated with a very powerful kind of archangelic contact. The vision was of a huge angel, with flame edged wings and a great sword, point downward, upon which he leaned. Then he raised the sword to point it directly at us, at the heart or solar plexus level. It was a tremendous spiritual contact. One felt all the inner muscular tensions going, rather like a super Alexander technique treatment. Then he lowered the sword and we felt at the same time a kind of dedication, protection, purification and encharging. Had to use the microscope technique to get down to normal consciousness afterwards.

There was a definite sense of a new phase of work starting, and indeed within a couple of months I had performed a working, based upon the circumnavigation of the world by Sir Francis Drake, that I felt at the time was the high point of my practical magical career and from the perspective of twelve years later it is still a major milestone in my esoteric development.

The HGW contact never returned and it seemed as if the job he had in mind had been done. I make no claims as to the validity of the identity of this contact. Wells was very much a rationalist in his day and so he came across on this occasion, only now as from the other side of the veil rather than this. He might well have been but a figment of our collective imagination that eventually melted, like Prospero's island "into air, into thin air." I only know that to make these things work you just have to take them at face value at the time, and that this "willing suspension of disbelief" pays handsome dividends. I am not in the least interested in wasting the powder and shot of argument with sceptics of no experience in these matters.

The contacts with angels and archangel and ancient Greek philosopher are simply reported as they appeared, without any claims as to having transcendental friends in high places. As with the figure of Wells one can only take the images at face value as they appear, whether or not they are masks being used by actors of another identity and dimension, or moving figures on a painted veil of one's own subjective higher consciousness. All of this can only be speculations of the intellect. The final arbiter is intuition and spiritual experience.

Any personal feelings as to the validity of this work lie not so much with the dramatis personae of this interior theatre, but with the contrast between the rather bored and even churlish reluctance in which we approached some of the meetings compared with some of the spiritual heights to which we felt raised towards the end, together with the very useful exercise in higher consciousness which anyone else is welcome to try.

It is my hope that the records of these imaginative workings, released from twelve years close confinement in my filing cabinet, may go forth and encourage others perhaps to take a first step in seeking similar adventures in wisdom or folly. After all they need no license or satellite dish - and the programmes to my mind are distinctly superior to what is currently available on terrestrial television.

4
MORE LIGHT ON THE WESTERN FRONT

"This lot wish to be known. They wish us to know such a brotherhood exists, and they exist to work for peace in a dynamic, strong, incisive way as an inner plane force who can be contacted and used to provide inspiration, initiative and push for peace and the environment". These words come from a Lodge report from a private working performed in July 1996, subsequently written up and published in *An Introduction to Ritual Magic* in a chapter explaining some of the purposes of magic. It would be a pity however if, in spite of this extended publicity, one of the vices of Malkuth should prevail, (Inertia), and nothing more be done about it.

Of course knowledge of this initiative will be restricted by the fact that the book is on a relatively specialist subject, and one that, thanks to lurid novels and occult works of popular vulgarity, is subject to some misunderstanding as to its intentions and practice. To the ignorant and thoughtless all magic is referred to as "black", in much the same way that all catholics are labelled "devout" and public holidays still called "bank".

Having nailed my colours to the mast some years back, I make no apology for retaining the dreaded "m" word, and indeed am rather fond of it. Forlorn hope that it may sometimes seem, I deem it no bad aspiration to try to restore some of the respect that the essentially noble Hermetic art deserves.

The subject has wider implications than is often realised. I was gratified to find that a clergyman with more than usual experience of mystical and psychical dynamics, to whom I sent a copy of the book, found no difficulty with my suggestion that a perfectly accurate alternative title could have been *An Introduction to Group Intercessory Prayer.*

He went on indeed to hail it as "a most successful double act ... which gave the whole thing a completeness and a character which it could not otherwise have had ... to represent a fulfilment of White Magic, a discovery of its right intention in that what is described is a desire to participate in the Divine Compassion which is what all true Intercession is all about."

This clergyman prepared me, many years ago, for confirmation into the Anglican church at a time when I was seeking to bring the Christian dynamic into magical practice without it becoming just another off-beat religious sect. He is thus not one to be fazed by unfamiliar terminology, perhaps through the Qabalistic insights he learned from me at the time, as the confirmation classes became very much a two-way process - a dialogue seeking common ground.

However, for most people the general problem remains. One would be as unlikely to find a book called *An Introduction to Intercessory Prayer* in an occult bookshop as to find *An Introduction to Ritual Magic* set out on a church bookstall.

As he went on to remind me, the making of conscious contacts with various discarnate characters, as described in relation to the inner Chapels of Remembrance, is no more than the Communion of Saints that is proclaimed in the creeds. It thus seems a bit odd for those who can psychically or intuitively perceive these fellow souls then to shy away from them as if they were "not quite nice"!

(Here the use of the term "saints" is in the Pauline tradition, as fellow members of the Body of Christ, rather than those of heroic virtue who have been duly canonised.)

Anyway, having opened up some form of contact that seems to represent some genuine need, we come to the question: "Where do we go from here?" This is hardly best answered by simply hoping that they will get fed up and go away. Better to invoke the well known adage for spiritual progress on the inner planes and "take the next step". In this case, since the reported event, the first steps that presented themselves have been taken. Indeed have become quite a number, that lead along various paths, albeit in the same general direction. The initial foray, it will be remembered, was centred on the area of the Somme, and in particular the town of Albert and its Golden Virgin. Subsequent steps have led to more northern sectors of the Western Front, in particular Ypres, Messines and Loos.

Loos

Loos is associated with Rudyard Kipling although I had not been aware of that when, in common with one or two other members of my group, I felt myself becoming increasingly conscious of him. This all started when one of our number felt drawn to construct quite an elaborate path working, structured upon a visit to Batemans, Kipling's 17th century home in Sussex. (This is also open to more prosaic visits, courtesy of the National Trust, and is well worth the trip.)

In the course of this working I experienced a more than usually powerful kind of personal contact when reading out a short passage in the character of Kipling. I felt as if his features were building over my own.

This is not an unusual kind of occurrence in spiritualist circles but was rather surprising to me in that my interpretation of Kipling's valedictory appeal, at the end of his collected poems, is a positive warning off to all meddlesome spirit mediums. "If I have given you delight by aught that I have done, let me lie quiet in that night which shall be yours anon: and for the little, little, span the dead are borne in mind, seek not to question other than the books I leave behind."

Whilst this is generally taken to refer to attempts at intrusive biography, which he used to refer to contemptuously as "the higher cannibalism", it also seemed to me an unequivocal occult "Keep Off" sign.

He was well aware of occult and psychic dynamics, even if he chose not to write about them too overtly, for he was aware also of their vulgar abuses. His father knew Madame Blavatsky well, his sister Alix was an active clairvoyant, and whatever his appreciation of the esoteric side of masonry may have been, his works are full of its symbolism.

In his autobiographical sketch *Something of Myself* he cites a most powerful and strange shared inner experience, on army manoeuvres near Aldershot in 1913, when it seemed as if all the dead of the Boer War were massing to give warning of some terrible disaster ahead. This was sufficient to cause even the hard-boiled army commanders to call short the manoeuvres, but Kipling never mentioned it until these posthumously published notes.

Following upon this initial evocation of Batemans however, I found that, as an abiding presence in the background of my consciousness, Kipling would just not go away. I therefore decided, with a certain amount of cautious reluctance, to embark on what was little more than a poetry reading in lodge. An occasion seemed to present itself in the centenary of the Diamond Jubilee of Queen Victoria. This occurred in August 1897 and was the cause of great junketing celebrating the ideals of Empire.

The imperialist ideal is not a particularly popular or politically correct subject these days, although like most human endeavours it had its bright as well as its dark side. Kipling was, and still is, popularly associated with being a keen advocate of it. His political image is painted somewhat to the right of Alf Garnett - to whom, by virtue of the moustache and rimless glasses, he bears a distinct physical resemblance. It is possible indeed, that when this television character of supreme and hilarious bigotry was created, Kipling was regarded as an appropriate physical role model.

However, such an identification is as grotesque as the fictional character itself. Kipling had a very demotic side to him. Not only did he have great empathy with the common British soldier, as demonstrated in *Barrack Room Ballads* but also with the Indian population, amongst whom he grew up as a young child, and with whom he mixed intimately as a newspaper reporter in Lahore and Allahabad, resulting in such stories as *Plain Tales from the Hills* and the immortal *Kim.*

On his rise to literary fame, and winning the Nobel Prize for Literature, he settled in the heart of the Sussex countryside and developed a deep understanding of the group soul of England and the spirit of the land. Encouraged by the example of his friend Edith Nesbit, who had found success with her magical childrens' novels capitalising upon her Hermetic Order of the Golden Dawn interests, he followed suit with *Puck of Pook's Hill* and *Rewards and Fairies,* a series of historical vignettes evoking the place memories of the English landscape through the evocation, "by oak, and ash and thorn" of one of the remaining Lords of the Hollow Hills.

However, on the occasion of Queen Victoria's Diamond Jubilee, he did not write a paean of imperial triumphalism, as had widely been expected of him. He contributed a poem, featured across the centrefold of the Times newspaper, entitled *Recessional;* which struck a new chord in the psyche of the nation. It sounded a note of warning that was to reverberate almost unheeded until the catastrophic explosion of imperial conflict in the 1st World War.

Even if Rudyard Kipling were anything of the imperial jingoist that he is sometimes made out to be, he paid for it in terms of personal suffering and remorse. His son John was only seventeen when war broke out, but anxious to join the colours, he tried to enlist, only to be twice turned down, as officer and as private, on account of his weak eyesight. His father however, as an old friend of Field Marshal Lord Roberts, managed to bend the rules, and secured him a commission in the Irish Guards. He also signed the papers of parental consent for his son, although still a minor, to go to France.

It was at the Battle of Loos in October 1915 that John Kipling lost his life. Not only that, his body was not recovered, having fallen in what for two years became No Man's Land. This was a terrible blow for Kipling, who spent years after the war vainly searching for his son's grave. Largely on this account he became a leading member of the War Graves Commission, and was responsible for the inscription upon the graves of all unidentified fallen soldiers "Known unto God".

He never did find his own son's grave, and was wracked with remorse for the rest of his life, and for the grief of his wife Carrie, feeling particularly responsible for the death of their child. Perhaps in consequence of this he became subject to bouts of acute stomach pain until the duodenal ulcers that had hitherto defied diagnosis caused his death in January 1936. Yet by a strange chain of circumstances, long after Rudyard Kipling's death, the grave of his son John was finally identified. His body had been recovered and interred in 1917 and had then been moved to another site in 1919, (a not uncommon practice after the war), as an unknown "lieutenant of the Irish Guards". From its original location, and close reference to regimental records, it was possible to identify this as the grave of John Kipling in 1994.

My intention, after the synchronistic coincidence of learning about all this in a magazine article at the appropriate moment, was to perform a very simple private ceremony of reciting selected poems culminating in the construction of a model grave with two handfuls of earth and some flowers, somewhat after the manner described in Kipling's poem *A Charm.*

However, things are never quite so simple or superficial when performed in magical circles. The occasion became a very powerful experience, as might be expected from the emotional intensity of some of the poetry, delivered to a small company each one of whom possessed a trained imagination.

On reciting the harrowing lines of *The Children* I felt as if the author had come very close to me. Indeed my voice took on a completely different timbre, similar in pitch to a recording of Kipling's voice that I later heard. However, such phenomena are but the incidental trivia of magical working. What was more important was that the event seemed somehow different from any normal magical ceremony.

Usually those upon the physical plane build up an imaginative and etheric vortex which those upon the inner planes then take away and work with, using it as a kind of lens in group consciousness akin to an astro/etheric communication satellite. On this occasion it seemed as if the flow were all the other way; that a vortex was being built up for us to take away and work with upon the physical level.

The focus for this fell particularly upon one of our number who, as described in the book, has been at the forefront of this kind of World War work. She felt impelled to wander into a nearby field, still very much in a state of tuned consciousness, where she picked up two handfuls of English soil, as described in *A Charm* and sang the version of Kipling's moving poem *Have You News of My Boy Jack?* which was set to music in 1917.

As she sang, it became clear to her what she had to do next. Experiencing a tremendous surge of energy, peace and well-being, she was prompted to take up a nearby cut log and run back with it up the hill. Then, once at home, she carved an epitaph upon it.

This took many hours to do in poker work with an old soldering iron, but it seemed appropriate to do it the hard way because the original makeshift grave crosses of the British army were done in this same laborious manner. The citation read: "John Kipling - in Remembrance of that Wind blowing and that Tide." Those who are familiar with the poem, or who take the trouble to look it up, will see the significance of these words.

It so happened that three of us were visiting war sites in France and Belgium the following week, albeit in the Ypres sector. However, a trip some miles south down the line to Loos seemed called for, to St. Mary's Advanced Dressing Station Cemetery where John Kipling lies.

It fell to me to lay the memorial offering upon John Kipling's grave, and it soon became apparent that this was not just a memento from a group of strangers and well wishers. By virtue of the contact that had recently been made the memorial was very much from Rudyard Kipling himself. My function was simply to provide the physical means by which he could fulfil what he had been unable to do himself in the flesh, all those years ago.

As in the poem *A Charm;* it took just two handfuls of earth to be scooped away to rest the log against the headstone. Already laid there, from a few days before, as in the poem, was a little bunch of wild flowers from his home village, inscribed "John Kipling, still remembered in Burwash, Sussex".

It also seemed important to walk slowly around the cemetery and impress it vividly upon my mind, including the landscape in which it stands, almost as if I were a mental camera. It so happened that I had the place to myself for the half-hour or so it took to do this, and found I was not lacking in companionship. Indeed I felt almost as if taken in as part of the family.

I have to say that I am at a loss to describe in terms of esoteric theory the inner significance of these events, beyond taking them in all due faith and sincerity at their face value. The initiative for it all seemed to come from the inner, although in terms of intellectual speculation I would not have thought that the departed spirit of Rudyard Kipling needed any sense of physical location of his son's body. Surely at least since 1936 they could have met each other in the world of spirit, so why this concern with past concerns in the world of the flesh?

It may be that in these actions we were helping to conclude some unfinished business on the part of some aspect of the soul of the long grieving father that could not otherwise rest. Or it might be that Rudyard Kipling, in his grief and close concern with the War Graves Commission had brought himself close to the group soul of the nation and of all grieving relatives of more than one war afflicted generation. In this sense we may have been performing some act of service for all those in a similar situation, of shattered relationships through barbarities of war, of whom that of John and Rudyard Kipling is a talismanic token in much the same way that Diana, Princess of Wales, focussed within herself some important dynamics of national and universal concern, that came to the surface and were released with incredible power at the time of her death.

Readers with Masonic connections may possibly understand more than me about any deeper significance in one of the entries in the cemetery visitors' book from members of "The Lodge of the Builders of the Silent Cities, Lille - founded by Rudyard Kipling". From experience so far it would seem that the denizens of these silent cities would like to make themselves heard!

Messines is a very small town, hardly bigger than a large village, that stands on a long, low ridge that overlooks the flat farmlands of Flanders in western Belgium, a few miles south of Ypres. It is a cluster of brick built houses in the Flemish style and a few small shops. In the centre the road to Ypres bends round in an S-shape before running straight along the top of the ridge on the line of the old Roman road.

Just off the second of these bends is a small town square with a compact stone church on the far side. This was once the site of a great medieval abbey, which was largely destroyed in the French revolution. In 1914 it was the scene of particularly bitter fighting when the invading German army occupied the ridge as a strategic point for attacking the British troops in the Ypres salient. It was from here that many of the shells were fired that destroyed the city of Ypres, and in turn the ridge was savagely fired on by British troops in an attempt to dislodge the Germans, resulting in the destruction of the whole town of Messines and many other villages along the ridge.

Eventually in 1916 the British army resorted to the desperate measure of tunnelling deep below the earth and planting unprecedented quantities of high explosives under the ridge. When the mines were detonated in 1917, at the start of what was to be called the Battle of Messines, the entire ridge was blown to pieces.

The remains of the ridge were then occupied by the British but were recaptured by the Germans after heavy fighting in the spring offensive of 1918, and then once more taken by the British in the autumn of that year. Although the town's church was destroyed, its 11th century crypt survived, and was used as an advanced dressing station for the wounded.

The town of Messines was rebuilt on the battle site after the war and a new church in the traditional style was built over the crypt. It was here, on a casual visit that had been intended as nothing more than a lunch stop, that we were approached by a local character, (appropriately named Albert for those who have synchronicities in mind,) who showed us over the place.

The crypt is particularly rich in history having been the last resting place of the mother of William the Conqueror and one of the monks of the abbey William of Messines became Patriarch of Jerusalem and Prior of the Holy Sepulchre (1130-45) in the days of the Crusader states. It is not without significance that he proved himself a force for conciliation in the troubled ecclesiastical and secular politics of his times. A more bizarre association is that an Austrian corporal of the German army was among those treated for wounds in the crypt, who later became better known as Adolf Hitler. As a British soldier, and winner of the V.C., who spared the life of the same wounded individual, had long cause to reflect, the quality of mercy makes no more distinction between the merits of individuals than the horrors of war.

At first glance this is a typical European church except that behind the tabernacle on the high altar is a row of flagpoles bearing the national flags of all the countries of Europe. There is also in the body of the church a statue of the Virgin Mary, crowned, that has been blessed by a visitation from the Pope. Another thing that catches the eye is a silver rose set into the wall, beside which is the photograph of a German officer. The rose, small but beautifully crafted, belonged to the old church of Messines. During the German occupation the church was looted and the silver rose taken by the German officer who took it home as a souvenir. Decades later, as an old man, he returned the rose to Messines where it now stands in the wall of the new church.

Also to be found within the crypt in a central alcove is one of the black madonnas that are found throughout Europe, often in crypts. The great cathedral of Chartres has one. Like so many of the others, this one too has an aura of ancient power and authority, a kind of counterpoise to the bright golden crowned madonna above.

On its site of an ancient crossroads, the church at Messines has become dedicated as a place of religious and political reconciliation between the nations. A carillon of bells is being constructed, with donations from all parts of the world. This is almost complete, and I was greatly honoured to be invited to play upon it, from a keyboard below. It seemed no small magical act, in the context of the current work, to send the notes of *Amazing Grace* ringing over the Flanders fields.

There is more work to come out of this, for the association of cross roads, silver rose, and bright and dark madonnas, has sparked a line of meditative work that seems to indicate some kind of linking of a Madonna of the Roses with the Rosicrucian Vault as a focus for a holy assembly of lights representing the group souls and their angels of all the nations of Europe.

Ypres

Ypres is a very attractive old Flemish town which has been reconstructed from being flattened after four years of bombardment during 1914-18. In the cathedral I lit a candle to one of the guardians of the Chapel of Remembrance mentioned in the book, (the cheeky one who was killed on the Ypres salient,) who responded in typical fashion by making the flame burn twice as high as any other candle present and then go into a minor firework display. This gentleman seems also to have theatrical ambitions as a way, not only of making himself better known, but as a means of forwarding the general drive of the work that is encapsulated in the inner Chapels of Remembrance. The theatre is not the most promising of media one would have thought, being always chronically short of cash with few opportunities for beginners, but he seems to have a way of making things happen. Hence the play, *This Wretched Splendour,* within a year had two productions, one amateur at the Playhouse, Cheltenham and one professional at the Grace Theatre, Battersea, of which Michael Billington, drama critic for *The Guardian,* wrote: "The standard first world war play is still R.C. Sherriff's Journey's End. But [this] knocks it into a cocked hat..." The script was subsequently published in the January 1999 edition of *Plays International.*

It also encouraged the Gloucestershire Red Cross to commission a play, with music, along similar lines, based upon local hospital records of the time, featuring the work of young volunteer nurses. The women's side of the war in ambulances, dressing stations and hospitals was no softer option than fighting in the trenches was for the men, to judge from contemporary accounts and the television programme *Roses of No Man's Land.*

It has been interesting to note, with regard to the play, how that strong inner plane involvement brings with it a spate of seemingly pointless coincidences. Thus the hero of *This*

Wretched Splendour; an officer named David from Coventry, was played by an actor whose name happened to be David and who also happened to come from Coventry. David was the name of the director too, and his surname of Wheeler evoked a light resonance with the regiment of the original protagonist - the Cycle Corps.

This kind of thing can have its uncomfortable side, as for example in the Kipling related work. Here all the concern with the business of tracing the missing body of a loved one was reflected in a much loved domestic cat going missing for a number of days, only to stroll back in alive and well after all the local vets and stray animal shelters had been needlessly alerted. Similarly, in synchronicity with John Kipling's last hours, I experienced tooth-ache and sensitivity of the teeth. Although the truth had been kept from Rudyard Kipling, who wrote a poem assuming that his son John died with a jest on his lips, in actuality he was last seen crying with the pain of a shrapnel wound in the mouth. I am happy to say that a visit to the dentist, including X-ray, revealed nothing wrong, and since the esoteric work has been completed the symptoms have gone. It seems important however to mention this rather unglamorous side to magical working as a cautionary note to those who aspire to unreserved dedication in this field.

This also raises some speculation as to the problems that inner plane contacts find in trying to direct the appropriate amount of force to bring things to our outer plane attention or to achieve specific results upon the physical plane. Some information along these lines was vouchsafed in the communication reported on pp.116-120 of *An Introduction to Ritual Magic.* A further interesting angle on this was demonstrated at an incident in the play's rehearsal. Let the playwright take up the story.

"In my play there is an Irish character who is supposed to be very psychic, and there's a scene in which he experiences a vision and comes out with a long and difficult monologue addressed to a recently killed comrade. The director wasn't happy with the actor's delivery of the monologue, so he asked me to help out by playing the "ghost" of the dead comrade, which basically meant standing a couple of feet in front of him, completely motionless, while he delivered the speech to me. Nothing very spectacular about this, it's a fairly standard technical exercise, based on the fact that it's easier for an actor to deliver a speech to a person than to a blank wall. But something started to happen. While I was standing there like a lemon being talked at, I felt an inner plane contact step into me. I felt myself becoming the dead soldier, and could feel my face changing - I felt the dried mud sticking to my legs and the weight of the pack and rifle, and the constriction of the tin helmet. I seemed to be bringing through a kind of fallen soldier archetype rather than a particular person, although it was using the character from the play as a template. It was a weird feeling, but the weirdest thing was the sense of viewing it all from the 'other side'. I felt that I was on the inner plane trying to communicate with someone on the outer, someone who was psychic enough to perceive me but only hazily, and standing in motionless silence I could feel the painful frustration of wanting the outer plane contact to understand but not being able to make him understand. My awareness of the rehearsal room and of the actor as himself almost disappeared, and I felt myself standing in the cold wet darkness, dead, trying to communicate with this living Irish bloke who knows I'm there, and who knows he's going to die too, and I'm trying to make him see what I see, which is the figure of the Golden Virgin streaming out redeeming light. And eventually he does see it, and the relief for both of us is indescribable. There's an extremely powerful vortex underlying the scene, which is of course why I wrote it in the first place, but it was extraordinary to have a really powerful magical experience in a theatre rehearsal - especially when I wasn't even acting, only being a prop to another actor. When he got to the end of the speech and I snapped back into myself I was in a right state - I was almost in tears and felt quite dizzy and disorientated. The actor told me afterwards that he'd had a very similar experience and had totally lost himself in the character until he wasn't aware of himself speaking the words. And the director was absolutely delighted! He was amazed at the power and conviction put into the speech. Let's hope he can do it like that on the night!"

Such involuntary magical experiences are not of course what is recommended in any responsible textbook upon the subject, but in magic as in war the textbooks do not always match up to the exigencies of practical experience in the field.

This does draw attention however to the power of the dynamic behind this work. As the report with which we commenced went on to say: "Approaching all this intellectually, I would have thought that there had been more than enough religious intercession and prayer for the soldiers of the world wars, but I fear that war being such an endless activity and generating so many countless casualties, there is a virtually ceaseless line of confused and tormented souls waiting to come through for healing etc., should an appropriate gate be opened."

To my mind the "etcetera" here covers a great deal of as yet unrevealed opportunity for service. Furthermore, as suggested in the book, it is no very great imaginative step to the inner recruiting office where the two officers described stand ready to offer the shilling to any who have the dedication to volunteer.

5
TREADING THE PATHS ON THE TREE

"Man, Know Thyself" was a motto emblazoned over the portal of the Delphic Oracle to sum up the whole human quest for higher knowledge and spiritual fulfilment. There are two other mottos that I would like to add to any portico of the Mysteries in modern times: "The Mind is Slayer of the Real" and "Fantasy is the Ass that carries the Ark." If these two injunctions were kept in mind by students of the ancient wisdom then the process of "getting to know themselves" would be the more rapid and less labyrinthine.

Putting this more succinctly, if we wish to make progress in the Mysteries we need to pay more attention to the imagination and less to the intellect.

Or, as a former Warden of the Society of the Inner Light, Arthur Chichester, was fond of saying, "Learn to go out of your mind." Then adding, as if by an after-thought, "But remember to come back to it!"

This is the time honoured and correct approach to the whole technique of working with symbolism. To find our way in this respect a simple analogy may be helpful. Let us visualise human consciousness in the form of a horse shoe magnet. The Spiritual Intelligence of higher consciousness and the Creative Imagination of lower consciousness are at each of the active poles, whilst the Intellect or Analytical Mind forms the unpolarised section of metal between them.

Our task as initiates is to irradiate our personalities with the inner light of spiritual intelligence, and the way we can achieve this is by a polar magnetic interchange between intuition and imagination, (the buddhic and the astral), by contemplation of noumenous symbols, which when held within the imagination are vehicles for spiritual realisation and contacts. We make a great mistake, on the other hand, if we try to puzzle away at these symbols with the unmagnetic analytical mind, which may have great merits on its own level when put to objective problems but is not best applied to things of the spirit.

Much of this should be obvious from the fact that religions of the world draw their strength from parables, or from stories (fictitious or otherwise) of their saints, rather than from theology. Similarly nations draw their moral strength from legends and stories of their heroes rather than from debates on the constitution. And back of all is the perenniel appeal of myths of the ancient world with their direct appeal to the imagination.

Our fore-runners in The Hermetic Order of the Golden Dawn were well aware of this approach to symbolism and its application to the Tree of Life in the technique that we nowadays call "path working." They were however prone to a mystagoguic streak which led them to call it by the somewhat portentous title of "scrying in the spirit vision", which tends to imply that it could only be performed by those gifted with some kind of mysterious psychic powers.

Yet nothing could be further from the truth. We are each and every one of us endowed with imagination, and all we need to "work the paths" or "scry in the spirit vision" is to learn how best to use it.

Unfortunately in the intellectual climate of our times it is often assumed that the imagination is little more than the vehicle for wishfulment fantasies, subjective escape mechanisms and general self deception. So it can be, but we would do well to remember the advice of the spiritual alchemists that the prima materia of the Great Work is everywhere, and overlooked and even despised because of it. That is to say, the creative imagination is the cornerstone of the temple that the builders have rejected.

When we apply these principles to the Tree of Life in Path working we use them to provide ourselves with the means of transposing consciousness from one level of inner awareness to another. These different levels or states of consciousness we refer to as Sephiroth, although I rather like to anglicise them as Spheres, for we can dress them imaginatively in any form that we wish without necessarily having recourse to Qabalistic theology.

One form of this can be in terms of the Arthurian Tradition, wherein Malkuth becomes the Forest of Broceliande, and Yesod the Lake in which the Faery Ladies educated some of the great heroes such as Lancelot, or brought the magic sword Excalibur to Arthur and subsequently received it back. Netzach may be seen as Camelot under the provenance of the Queen to which she brought the Round Table that was her dowry through the provenance of Merlin. Hod on the other hand could be the more militant castle of Caerleon and starting point of adventures for errant knights, whilst beyond the mystic mountains the Grail Castle might be located in Tiphareth. The Paths then become the forest ways of various adventures from one location to another.

This is but one scenario, which is described in a little more detail in *"The Secret Tradition in Arthurian Legend,"* not that I claim much originality for it, as it stems from pioneering psychic work jointly embarked upon by Dion Fortune and Maia Tranchell-Hayes in 1941. It circulated for many years in typescript form as the *Arthurian Formula* until eventually through the course of events I simply became the cup bearer for it to the outer world. The fact that it took until 1983 to make the transition into published work, some 42 years, (with a further 14 years for American, French and Italian editions) gives some indication of how slowly the mills of God can grind when it comes to disseminating arcane wisdom to the outer world. Or perhaps we should be less inclined to hide our light so secretively under a bushel.

Let me say that the *Arthurian Formula,* unique as it is in many respects, is but one form in which an imaginative approach to the Mysteries can take, and other myths and legends could be similarly utilised, for the Tree of Life is a universal structure, a framework upon which many forms of mythopoeic imagination can be hung.However, in the more formal working of the Paths of the Tree of Life we use a triple convention of symbolism, an amalgam of three separate traditions: A Trump from the Tarot, a letter from the Hebrew alphabet, and a symbol from Astrology. Each of these elements is as a seed that we plant within the rich soil of the creative imagination.

Each is capable of sprouting forth an enormous range of association of ideas. It is this teeming complexity that gives them their great evocative strength and power and capacity for inter-relationship. Yet at the same time this profound prolixity can lead us into a deadly trap - the quagmire of intellectual speculation. A quagmire that solidifies like concrete around our feet if we should start turning speculation into theory or even ultimately into dogma.

Dogma is not the exclusive preserve of theologians, it is the defence mechanism of those who crave for certainty. It occurs in any area of debatable knowledge. The more that facts are capable of alternative interpretations, the more rigid and fanatical is dogmatic theory likely to become. We see it in the arts, and in "soft sciences" such as psychology, economics, political theory, and of course not least in the esoteric world. As evidence of this, consider how much heart searching and burning the midnight oil has been expended over such issues as the "correct" attributions of the various symbolic correspondences.

Let me pass on a grisly secret. There is no set of correspondences that is the one and only truth!. There may be some that are better than others in particular circumstances, but the one that is best is the one that works for you. This is likely to be the one you happen to have been trained in, but it does not mean that others are wrong.

In evidence of this we have only to extend our vision beyond our own backyard. The Qabalistic attributions used by the French, deriving from Eliphas Levi, are different from those used by the English speaking world, deriving from the Golden Dawn, simply because they choose a different numerical order for placing the Tarot Trumps. Yet is anybody going to tell me that all Francophone Qabalistic occultism is ineffective, or alternatively all Anglophone? Certainly in my various lectures in England or in France I have found one or two so bigoted as to think so, but my acquaintance with English or French speaking occultists has not led me to the conclusion that either has any less claim to effectiveness and wisdom than the other.

What is more, recent historical research by Professor Michael Dummet and others demonstrates that there is no universally accepted order for the Tarot Trumps. We can therefore apply whatever system fits our purpose. Nonetheless I have found that the Golden Dawn system suits me well enough, although this has not prevented me from a little experimentation on the side. In fairness to the more conservative, it is probably best to specialise in one particular system, even if arbitrarily chosen, rather than pick and mix in the eclectic fashion of the experienced adept. But we should not sneer at others who may have elected to work a different set of attributions, that's all.

The crux of the matter is that at the back of all legend and myth is the desire to tell or listen to a story. In the context of Path working we are simply being invited to make up and tell a story, either to ourselves, or to other people. This is no more than any junior or infant school teacher is expected to do by way of training and function, and is perhaps one reason why school teachers often make very good magicians. Better certainly than actors, who tend to feel lost unless someone has provided them with a script.

There is no great difficulty in making up our own script for Path working, even as we go along, because the traditional symbols provide us with a skeleton outline. The ancillary characters and objects in our story are then provided by the rich and varied associations that are evoked when we call any of the key symbols to mind.

Many of these associations we can read up on intellectually beforehand by study of relevant books but as we gain confidence with practice we will begin to find that other associations spring into consciousness spontaneously, that we may not even have considered beforehand. This is a red letter occasion, for it means that we are directly accessing our own spiritual intelligence.

There are critics more opinionated than experienced who have taken it upon themselves to condemn path working as being merely an arcane form of psycho-analysis, dumping personal subconscious complexes upon a captive audience. Certainly techniques of free fantasy have their place in certain forms of psychotherapeutics, but in the context of the Mysteries we are dealing with selected noumenous symbols upon an objective metaphysical framework. Therefore in practice there is considerable difference between the tuning of higher consciousness by the initiate, and the personal inspection of lower consciousness by the psychotherapist.

For successful Path working we need sufficient preparation in the longer and the shorter term. By the shorter term we mean having read up on the immediate associations of the symbols of the Path for two or three days previously. By the longer term we mean a goodly period of time meditating and otherwise working upon the Tree of Life in general. This is the function of formal training within the Lesser Mysteries.

Taking copious notes and even writing them out in the form of a script does not however constitute a Path working. It is only the preparatory homework for one. Path working itself is like a magical performing art. It is an occasion that happens once, in a particular place at a particular time with a particular group and with particular inner tides at work. It is done without a written script so that the operator can react flexibly to the balance between the inner and the outer conditions. In this respect it is similar to taking a scripted ceremonial office, but without the structured force flows of a ritual. There the officers react and polarise one with another and with the inner powers they represent. In a Path working the operator polarises directly and spontaneously with the group, both inner and outer.

Not having a script is a relief rather than a burden. Where there is nothing pre-ordained there can be no mistake or deviation from it. Lines that are not written down cannot be fluffed or forgotten.

Memory plays little part in the matter, despite the number of words that may be uttered. Or no more than the ability to recall the five symbolic stages of the Path. Sphere of Origin. Tarot Trump. Hebrew Letter. Astrological Sign. Sphere of Destination. Any other objects, characters or events come up automatically by free association.

In basic structure it is only a simple narrative journey. We do not, like a novelist or dramatist, have to cast it into a complex series of exciting crises. We simply start at one state of consciousness exemplified by a scene in a Sphere, and make our way by three steps to our destination, whereupon we simply turn round and return by the way we went. The natural sequence of prescribed seed symbols, together with the stated will and intention of the operation at the commencement, should do the necessary trick of raising consciousness from one state or sphere to the other.

In ancient memory systems, used by orators who did not wish to risk the deadening effect of reading from a prepared script, and which are particularly associated with Rosicrucian writers such as Robert Fludd, a sequence of inner locations was chosen in which various points to be recalled were imagined to be. From this we get the origin of the phrase "in the first place... ", "in the second place..." followed each time with points of argument.

A structured Path working is a simple form of this method. The various places being the three principal symbols allocated between the start and the finishing point. Calling the symbols to mind will evoke all that one has studied about them in the past, and indeed, and here experience will prove convincing and illuminating, related ideas that have gathered in a common pool, either from the previous mediations of others throughout the ages, or from one's own bank of evolutionary memories, or from the intimations of inner plane contacts whose presence we may not have hitherto realised. It is for this reason that Path working is a capital form of spiritual and magical training.

In the first place we have a Tarot Trump, one from a great common stock of images in the general pool of consciousness. We do not have to be limited by what we may have read in esoteric books on the Tarot. Some of the images have much wider application, particularly if we look at patterns of very old cards. Thus the card of the Chariot does not only have Egyptian or male characteristics, which are largely a 19th century French introduction, but goes right back to the ancient and female winged Victory, which will lead on to a whole range of other associations. Similarly the Wheel of Fortune originally had the goddess Fortuna turning it, banished presumably by the need for medieval woodblock carvers to try to simplify an already complex design. Whilst the mystery of the dog and wolf on the Trump of the Moon receives some clarification from the common French expression "entre chien et loup" to signify the time of Twilight, an alternative title for the card. Any of these alternatives give considerable scope and stimulus to the magical imagination.

In the second place we have the Hebrew Letter. There is perhaps more "authority" for the placement of these than for the other symbols insofar that their allocation comes from the ancient Qabalistic text the *Sepher Yetzirah.*

It is possible in this context to become lost in a maze of medieval Jewish number mysticism and here I would advise caution and draw attention to the vast gap between the assumptions and indeed the aims of medieval Jewish Qabalism and the post Renaissance Christian Qabalah that is our immediate heritage. Something of the difference in conception may be gathered from a remark of Professor Gershom Scholem, one of the great experts on Judaic mysticsm who, in *Major Trends in Jewish Mysticism,* writes off our version of the Qabalah as so much "highly coloured nonsense".

He is of course probably no great expert in our preferred line of "nonsense" but nonetheless there is obviously a considerable abyss to be bridged before any meaningful dialogue can take place. However, ever since Pico della Mirandola offered to convert the Jews by use of their own Qabalistic texts, there has been a tradition of Gentiles raiding Jewish mystical wisdom and using it for their own purposes, even through gross distortion and misunderstanding of it.

As a pragmatist I am of the view that if something works then why not use it, rather than worry about someone else's theory. After all, I am told that if a bumble bee had studied aerodynamics it would realise it could not fly. Yet in ignorance of the theory it manages to do so quite well.

With this in mind I simply take the meaning of the Hebrew Letter and elicit what I can from that, bearing in mind that the original symbol stems from a very ancient culture. Therefore an ox, which is associated with the letter Aleph, means very much a driving power, for the ox was the motive power that drew the plough and drove the mill and water pump and pulled the cart to market, and if the ancient Jews or their orthographical forebears had been blessed with modern technology they might well have put a tractor or internal combustion engine here. In short, Aleph has associations as a power source, which coming straight out of Kether on the 11th Path seems no bad allocation.

This would not prevent me from drawing an association across to the stellar constellation of Taurus, the bull, and all the resonances that that this might carry, from some of Zeus's affairs with legendary maidens, to ancient Egyptian reverence for the Apis bull, even the bovine associations of Isis, Io, Europa or even Pasiphae. One can see that this kind of symbol juggling would be to Professor Scholem rather like the golden calf was to Moses, let alone the red rag to a bull, but what may legitimately seem nonsense to him may well be the divine wisdom of the Fool to me.

The moral then, I think, is to take what seems useful from other traditions, hold fast to that which is good for our own understanding, and not be shackled or misled by that which is not.

These considerations apply also to the so-called Yetziratic Text for each Path, which have an importance in our preparation in that they are held to embody the Intelligence of the Path, or what one might call its angelic oversoul. They can certainly can have an evocative resonance, but whether this is helped or hindered by the obscurity of some of the language, and what sometimes seems to be no more than ham fisted translation, is open to question. Personally, rather than learn it off by heart and unleash it upon an uncomprehending audience I make a personal gloss of it according to my own understanding.

Then at least if I have got it all wrong according to the original rabbinic authority's intention, it makes sense to me, and by extension, one hopes, to those whom I am addressing.

And in the third place in our Path working we have the Astrological sign, which may be one of the twelve signs of the zodiac or of the traditional astrological planets plus three of the Elemental signs, although for the latter one might, if one is adventurous, perhaps try substituting the extra-Saturian planets of Uranus, Neptune and Pluto.

There is an enormous astrological literature available here, probably far more extensive than even the exegesis of Hebrew letter and number mysticism, or works on the Tarot. This is yet further increased if one takes into account the god and goddess forms and attributions of the planets and zodiacal signs. There is a whole range of "starry wisdom" here that should prove of service to even the most stolidly unimaginative path worker.

These three steps that we have reviewed take us naturally into the Sphere at the further end of the Path. Take what you can of the atmosphere here, expressing it in symbolic terms of place or person, then you can return to the place from whence you started. This can be quite cursorily done, simply as a technical exercise in psychological association of ideas, returning to the original state of consciousness in business like and no nonsense fashion. When you have gained a little skill however, and perhaps with a little help from any friends you may have gained upon the inner planes, you may find that the return journey can be as evocative and rewarding as the journey out - for now you return bringing back the sheaves of realisation, whereas you set out simply with the seeds of aspiration.As an appropriate peroration on the importance of the imagination, and daring, willing and knowing how to use it, I would draw attention to an early address within our archives from one upon the inner planes who masterminded *The Cosmic Doctrine* through the mediumship of Dion Fortune on 11th October 1925. It may have been on the files for seventy odd years but it is none the less true and appropriate for us now, particularly as its recommendations, apart from their intrinsic value, can also be applied to Path working.

"Greeting, my children. Have you yet become familiar with the inner planes? Use the picture method. Try and see us. It makes us so much more real, and when we are real to you we can talk to you so much more easily. It is by building a form on the astral that we contact you. That form has hitherto been built by the consciousness of the transmitter, but if you could build composite forms with the group consciousness you would obtain more definite results, and when each one of you has become accustomed to building a picture in consciousness in group meditation, and of hearing the sound of the voice, you would soon find that you are able to build that form in solitary meditation and hear the voice in your inner consciousness; and the more to whom we can thus speak, the stronger will the group be."

"You will have many problems to solve in the course of your work, but one thing you must always guard, and that is your belief in the Masters, for without that you can do nothing. It is your contacts with them that are the source of your powers as a group, but it is highly desirable that each one of you shall learn to hear for yourselves the voices within, and for that purpose we shall work upon you and visit you individually, and you must try and hear us. You must listen for us and reach out towards us. Visualise us one by one, and call upon us and try to hear the answer. Thus shall you make the contacts for yourselves. For we are real. We are what we claim to be, and the proof lies in the power. If you doubt that power, invoke it and watch it work. When you come to these meetings come in faith, for it is your faith that makes the communication possible, and without it we cannot come through."

"Reach back into your past lives and try to remember seeing the scenes and yourself as moving among them. This is a valuable exercise for waking the higher faculties. You must become to dare greatly, and to trust your own psychism. The images rise dimly at first and are elusive, but not illusory. Learn to look at the fleeting images as they form and disappear and with practice you will be able to hold them steady. Remember that it is the imagination that is trained. It is with the imagination, that is to say, the power of visualising that the form is built in astral matter which we use as material for contacting you."

"Whenever you think of the Masters you touch them, you lay the hand of your soul upon them. It is very necessary for the work that the Masters should frequently be with those who may be an open channel for communication, therefore we shall often come and talk to you about simple things, and about your life, so that we may get to know each other."

So much for assumptions that the Masters are so elevated that they have no time to spare for their own servers and will only come through their seniors!

Nor it would appear is the ability to be a trance medium necessary. Another communicator of those times, a rather impressive visitor described as "an Agent of the Lords of Karma", expressed the view that communications of the future

75

would not be done through trance mediumship but "through trained Initiates with full consciousness."

With the natural passage of time since then, it may well be assumed that THIS MEANS YOU!

6
AWEN – THE POWER
IN THE MAGICAL CAULDRON

When we speak of magic we do not mean a bizarre indulgence in some fantasy world that promises to provide some means of escape from reality. Nor do we mean a mental toolkit to gain power or influence over others by dubious methods of applied psychology. True magic is something that lies at the very heart of human consciousness and the expression of the human spirit in an evolving universe.

Some of the subject matter of true magic may seem somewhat strange when we come upon it for the first time. Yet as we progress, certain topics turn up again and again, regrouping in various ways. These recurring topics refer to a complex of mysteries that includes concepts such as:

a) the place of the Earth among the Stars,

b) Power within the Land,

c) Divine and Sacrificial Kingship,

d) the Poetic Inspiration of the Bard,

e) the Principle of Sovereignty.

Our use of capital letters signifies that we mean something rather more than is commonly implied by these astronomical, cultural or geophysical terms.

Some of these ideas might seem easier to understand if put in psychological terms. We might regard them, say, as structures of archetypes in the collective unconscious – whether of races or of nations, or ultimately of humanity as a whole. After all, the terms of psychology are more familiar to most modern readers than those of ancient magic.

However, although psychology may give a rough approximation of what true magic is all about, its assumptions tend to promote some serious misunderstandings. For in terms of magic, psychological labels are at best half-truths. They confine us to a self-imposed "psycho-sphere" that is itself the product of physical brain consciousness. A prison house of the skull – a veritable Golgotha wherein the human spirit is crucified.

When we speak of magic we speak of a far wider world, and not one that is simply subjective, or even telepathically shared. The psychic and spiritual worlds are supremely objective – as objective as the Earth itself. As objective as its rivers, lakes, seas and mountains, and the stars and planets in the vibrant space that surrounds the globe in which we live and move and have our being.

The physical shell of the universe is investigated, catalogued and manipulated by physical science and technology. But resonating within and beyond it are the psychic and spiritual worlds that embody consciousness in many different modes and forms.

These concern not only the psychic and spiritual elements of the human, animal, vegetable and mineral kingdoms but extend into realms that may commonly be regarded as fantasy.

They have their ancient roots of exposition in folklore and in myth – which are none the less potent today, presented through popular fiction via the media. They are preserved in traditions embracing our own ancestors, whether near or remote in time; in tales of the worlds of faery, "the lordly ones" who dwell in the hollow hills; and in religious beliefs incorporating heavenly messengers and angelic choirs.

There is nothing new in any of this. It is no recently hatched fantasy fiction. Beneficent beings and spirits of nature and of the starry firmament were well known to the ancients, and it was by a strange quirk of human nature that the medieval church elected to demonise them. Unfortunately, in our cocksure faith in the wonders of science and technology, we have gone to the other extreme. With sceptical rationality we have very efficiently banished them.

This does not mean that these wondrous realms have been destroyed. It simply means that we have adopted the defence mechanisms of the ostrich and voided them from our own sight and consciousness. The discipline of magic is a means of withdrawing our heads from the sand and looking around at a wider world. Hopefully, even communicating with it.

Communication, however, requires a common language. The vocabulary of which is contained in the characters, objects and events of myth and of legend, or in metaphysically loaded symbols. Much of what is left of the ancient commerce between the worlds is now fragmented folklore. It is as if a once universal language remains only in isolated pockets of local dialect. Is this perhaps the true meaning behind the story of the tower of Babel and the confusion of tongues?

There have been many attempts to fashion some kind of common language between the outer and inner worlds. One example is to be found in alchemy. In particular the acrostic VITRIOL to represent the idea of a "universal solvent". It stands for "Visita Interiora Terrae Rectificando Invenies Occultum Lapidem" which we might render as "Visit the interior of the Earth to find and rectify the hidden stone."

Even so this may be difficult for us to comprehend, confined as we are within our concrete intellectual bunker. Nonetheless, the solidity of the concrete is gradually crumbling. Some have deplored this tendency as "a flight from reason". However the flight is one of eagles not of fugitives. We do not seek to escape from reason, but merely to put it in its proper place. To see it as a mental tool whose use may be better understood from a higher and wider perspective.

There is a useful Celtic term that pertains to this: "Awen" – which might be translated as Inspiration. In its fullness however, it is untranslatable in a single word. It signifies a kind of irradiation of the soul from paradisal origins, which in turn depends on what we may understand by Earthly or Heavenly Paradise.

Our descriptions and definitions can only be rendered in poetic terms. Hence the importance of the Bard. And in bardic language the source from which this Awen or inspiration rises is the Cauldron of the Underworld, of Annwyn, or, in alchemical terms, "the interior of the Earth".

This has its later cultural manifestation as the Holy Grail. In classical times it saw the sun god Apollo surrounded by the Nine Muses around the Pierian Spring. Apollo also, of course, was patron of the oracle at Delphi, to which the wisdom of inspiration ascended from the inner earth, emanating from a dragon power. The dragon, known as Ladon, originated in the far west, to which various heroes went in search of various inspirational treasures that were kept by various guardians, from the head of the Medusa, to the golden apples of Atlanta. There are many ways by which we may approach this fount of inspiration. Indeed, left to the speculations of the concrete mind, they may seem to lead us only into an encyclopedic labyrinth.

Yet an Ariadne's thread to lead us to the source has been preserved in the Celtic folk soul. This is not the only vehicle of inner wisdom, but nonetheless is one of the most evocative guardians of the lost and ancient tradition.

The Celts provide an immediate bridge that leads to a very ancient world. They preserved much of the traditions of the Bronze Age beaker people, and beyond them of the Neolithic builders of stone and wooden circles and burial mounds. Behind these, yet again, some believe there to be an even more ancient wisdom – derived, it is conjectured, from the lost world of Atlantis. The existence of that world may not conform to modern scientific theories but scientific theories do not extend to the provinces of Annwn.

At the same time it was Celtic bards who laid the foundation for the knightly legends of the high middle ages. Most of what has come down to us as Arthurian Tradition was seeded by Celtic bards who, leaving Wales and Cornwall for Brittany, after the Saxon invasions, sought service with Frankish lords, and provided the tales that informed the Arthurian romancers of the twelfth and thirteenth centuries.

Chrétien de Troyes, Robert de Boron and others, wove them into tales of Merlin, Arthur, Lancelot and Guenevere, the Lady of the Lake and the Questors of the Grail. Later Sir Thomas Malory rendered these tales in Old French into the English tongue, his works being one of the first great volumes from Caxton's printingpress. So if we find our imagination stimulated by Arthurian tales, we may get closer to their origins by a studying their ancient roots, and the Celtic inspiration which lies directly behind the medieval French.

Fortunately no knowledge of ancient Welsh is required, thanks to Lady Gregory, who translated what has become known as *The Mabinogion,* and to later scholars for surveying the ground with more scholarly vigour. Furthermore, many clues have been given us as to where to pan for true gold in these remote mountain streams of wisdom.

We may cite Robert Graves, (*The White Goddess*), R.J.Stewart, (*The Underworld Initiation, Earth Light, Power within the Land, The Prophetic Vision of Merlin* etc.), Caitlín Matthews, (*Mabon and the Mysteries of Britain, Arthur and the Sovereignty of Britain,* etc.), John Matthews (*Taliesin*), and most recently *Awen, the Quest of the Celtic Mysteries* by Mike Harris, who presents an account derived from magical field work in his native Snowdonia.

Despite its cosmic resonances, it is not a tradition of remote metaphysical abstractions. It speaks in terms of the relationship of people to the land upon which they live. It speaks of the inspired songs and stories of the minstrels and the bards. It speaks of great kings and heroes. It speaks of wondrous hallows and consecrated objects. It speaks moreover of the powers of the inner Earth and the hollow hills. Of the faery tradition. Of the Earth's relation to the stars. Above all it speaks of the great game of life played out on the chequer board of daily experience, known as the chess like game of

Gwyddbwyll, (approximately pronounced as *gweeth-buth*), which also signifies the land.

The general public has an intuitive realisation of the current importance of these things. This is largely undefined, coming through instinctive channels. It is expressed in cultural terms by the explosion of interest in stone circles and other ancient sites. Time was when I can remember visiting Stonehenge and having the place to myself; likewise Avebury. No chance of that now! Stonehenge is surrounded by barbed wire and concrete fortifications containing turnstiles, toilets and tourist shops.

Fortunately it is not essential to confine one's esoteric interests to famous sites. There are many other places of power, untouched by commercial exploitation. The important point is that the universal may well be found within the locality, even, if you are lucky, within your own back yard.

This is simply a down to earth demonstration of the philosophical axiom that the microcosm is a reflection of the macrocosm. In its ultimate sense, this is to see the world in a grain of sand, as the modern bard William Blake proclaimed. Less rigorously, a postage stamp of land can contain the pattern of the greater universe. A recent book, *The Star Mirror,* (by Mark Vidler, Thorsons 1998), has analysed this in relation to the pyramids of Gizeh and the stars of Orion, amongst other locations and constellations. Mike Harris has found similar effects in the lakes and mountains of Wales.

Much the same local discovery was made by the pioneer anthropologist W.Y. Evans Wentz. He crossed the American continent and the Atlantic Ocean to research *The Fairy Faith in Celtic Countries.* Having produced this book he proceeded to the Himalyas, and over thirty years established himself as a world authority on Tibetan Buddhism with translations and commentaries on *The Tibetan Book of the Dead* and other major texts. In the evening of his days he went back to the place whence he had started, and found wisdom back home in San Diego county, California, on Cuchama, a local sacred mountain. Yet this is no parochial matter, the focus is universal.

Many things that seem unique in one presentation of the mystery tradition, may be reflected in another. Let us take, for example, a strange sequence from *The Chymical Wedding of Christian Rosencreutz,* that strange literary jewel in the crown of the Rosicrucian mysteries.

A King and a Queen are about to be beheaded but attend a celebration before a central altar, upon which there stand a celestial globe, turning of its own volition, a striking clock, a crystal fountain of liquid the colour of blood, and a skull containing a white snake. The snake is so long that it can encircle all the other objects whilst its tail remains in one of the eyeholes and its head returns to the other. Yet it may be caused to appear and disappear according to the ministrations of a little god of love, Cupid, the son of the goddess Venus.

We may find much the same symbolic artefacts within the Celtic mysteries. Mike Harris, for example, in *Awen, the Quest of the Celtic Mysteries* can devote a chapter to Cauldron, Grail, Skull and Snake.

It may seem strange that there is common ground between the symbolism contained within a 17th century Rosicrucian text and these ancient Celtic traditions but the fundamentals of the true mysteries remain the same throughout all time. It is only the detail of their presentation to human understanding that changes, according to the vagaries of cultural history.

Let us demonstrate this with a simple diagram, from which the complex may be rendered simple. The objective of true magic is to provide a matrix for interaction between the Material and the Spiritual worlds. We can represent these two worlds, each by a circle that just touch tangentially at a single point. The Material World might also be called the world of growth, or "becoming", of time and space; and the Spiritual World the world of "archetypal being" of eternity, of the divine mind.

Between them we construct a third circle, whose circumference touches both their centres, and so also links them. This third circle is a sacred space, called by the Celts Annwyn, (pronounced *anoon*) and it contains Awen, or Inspiration. In pictorial imagery it was therefore seen as a cauldron, either of the goddess Keridwen, or of the great giant Bran the Blessed, or the Irish father of the gods, the Dagda. As such it is situated at the central point of Annwn and may be surrounded by three times three goddesses or faery maidens or, in the case of the ancient Greek version, the nine muses of the Sun god.

Awen, we have said, is somewhat inadequately translated as Inspiration. It represents all the powers within the cauldron, within the sacred space between Heaven and Earth, which are also known as waters of Regeneration, or of Transformation. In various traditions it is a mass of potential, whose substance has been known as the sperm of the all-father god, as the milk of the goddess, as star-dust, or as the bloodless death – that is to say, initiation.

To play the game of destiny, or of sovereignty (of the land as sacred king, or of oneself), is also the work of true magic, which is to provide patterns in consciousness or ritual action through which the Awen may take substance, and implant spiritual ideas into physical reality.

The pattern upon the land, or within the magic circle, or within the cauldron, may be made up by specific nodes that we can designate upon our diagram in a seven-fold manner. In the Celtic mysteries they are the seven Caers of Annwyn but they have their correspondence in other magical systems. The closer such Caers are to the Spiritual world we have to do with angelic magic and cosmic powers and the starry wisdom; the closer they are to the Material world we have to do with etheric magic, the planetary being, the wild herdsman, and elemental beings.

Powers within the cauldron or the sacred space may appear in various guises. As guardians, porters, guides, monsters, giants, dragons, knights, kings, queens, maidens, vavaseurs, magicians, enchantresses, hermits, faery women.

Those who are trained in Qabalah will find themselves on familiar ground if they see the nodal points as Spheres upon the Tree. The central circle is then revealed as the "magical circuit" of Daath/Yesod with the Supernal Triad representing the Spiritual world above and the Sephirah Malkuth the Material world below.

For those who are students of *The Cosmic Doctrine* the diagram can be applied to the chapter on the Law of Impaction and Transmission of Action from One Plane to Another.

Far from being metaphysical speculation, much of this can have an immediate and frightening relevance. There are some very modern exemplars of the bardic tradition, who have undergone similar experiences to the Scottish Merlin, driven temporarily insane and thence to bardic inspiration by the horrors of war. We could mention Alun Lewis and Robert Graves, Robert Owen and Siegfied Sassoon, C.S. Lewis and Tolkien.

A similar tale is to be found wherever a decay of sovereignty leads to a waste land, when the Spiritual and Material worlds lose contact. What happened on the Somme or at Ypres, in Auschwitz or Belsen, in Korea, Vietnam, Bosnia or today on the streets of Northern Ireland, are of the same dynamic as the ancient strife of tribes in Caledonia or of Arthur's last battle against Mordred.

The Maimed King and the Waste Land have their counterparts repeated in history as the corruption of sovereignty and of the land that goes with it. It occurred particularly significantly with the leper king Baudouin IV, of the Crusader Kingdom of Jerusalem, contemporary with Chrétien de Troyes, whose fate has a strange parallel with the maimed king of the Wasteland in *Le Conte du Graal*. The search for Awen therefore remains a relevant and urgent need. Like the hidden stone of the philosophers it is frequently overlooked, despised and rejected. But it remains the only bridge whereby the land, and that implies the whole body of the Planetary Being of Earth, may be healed. Like Percivale, we have to learn to ask the right questions, then the answers may be forthcoming.

7

QABALAH AND THE OCCULT TRADITION

In my own particular Quest during this life I find I have been studying the Occult Tradition for exactly as long as I have been studying Qabalah, for in the school in which I was trained, the terms were regarded as largely synonymous.

However that is not necessarily the case. There are many occultists who are not Qabalists, just as there are many Qabalists who are not occultists. Anyhow, I am one, through historical accident, who can lay claims to both. So when I enrolled in Dion Fortune's occult school, the Society of the Inner Light, 45 years ago, it was upon her version of Qabalah that I was trained. If my pronunciation of certain terms differs slightly from those that you are used to, it is because they were those adopted by Dion Fortune. One of the useful facets of Qabalism is that you can usually tell someone else's antecedents from the type of mis-spelling and mis-pronunciation they use.

Well, who was Dion Fortune and what claims does she have to be occultist or Qabalist? Her great asset, which many students like me appreciate, is that she wrote one of the most lucid texts in English upon the Qabalah from an occult point of view. *The Mystical Qabalah* was written as articles in The Inner Light Magazine during the early 1930's, was published in book form in 1935, and has remained in print ever since.

Thirty years later, as a member of her school I wrote a follow up work, *A Practical Guide to Qabalistic Symbolism,* more as a supplement to Dion Fortune's work, rather than with any intent to replace it.

We should also acknowledge the work of Israel Regardie, who in 1937 put into the public domain most of the Knowledge Papers of the Hermetic Order of the Golden Dawn – which remain a reference source for many Qabalistic occultists to this day – and have provided a core of practical material for various revivalist groups as far afield as the United States, South Africa and New Zealand.

Israel Regardie and Dion Fortune represented in their works a new generation of useful and readable occult and Qabalistic textbooks. They knew each other quite well and, from correspondence I have seen, seem to have struck creative sparks off each other.

They were both quite excited about Jungian psychology, which was becoming well known at this time, and which influences Regardie's books to some extent, although he later became a Reichian therapist. Somewhat confusingly, his book upon the Tree of Life is called *The Garden of Pomegranates,* and his book entitled *The Tree of Life* is mainly about magic. His other Qabalistic work, *The Middle Pillar,* was also important for its eminently practical approach.

Dion Fortune and Israel Regardie both descended from the same occult and Qabalistic school, that is to say the Hermetic Order of the Golden Dawn. They were not the only ones of course. There were a number of others who made their mark upon the esoteric scene, including the somewhat notorious Aleister Crowley, the American Paul Case, whose Golden

Dawn temple in Chicago went on to become a respected occult school that is still going today, the Builders of the Adytum, specialising in Tarot applications to the Tree of Life and the Cube of Space of the Sepher Yetzirah. Others were famous in other fields of activity, such as the poet W.B. Yeats or the novelists Brodie Innes and Algernon Blackwood, the writers of childrens' books E. Nesbit and even P.L. Travers, the creator of Mary Poppins, who came under its influence via Yeats. His friend and fellow Golden Dawn member George Russell, (who wrote under the pen name of AE) considered that Mary Poppins was very much the incarnation of an ancient tutelary goddess. Whether Julie Andrews, in the Walt Disney film, quite measures up to this conception is another matter.

The detailed teaching of the Golden Dawn was largely the brain child of an extremely dedicated man Samuel Liddell MacGregor Mathers, who spent much of his time in the British Museum Reading Room making a conflation of occult and Qabalistic traditions. The Golden Dawn, established in 1888, was the result of his synthesising abilities. He has been saddled with the reputation of being something of an autocrat although I think this may be something of an injustice. If there were any organisational problems with the Golden Dawn I think they are likely to have occurred from a lack of discipline rather than a surplus of it. And the formation of a number of largely self governing branches of the Order and his own removal to Paris to set up a temple there, do not suggest to me a control freak. He died in Paris in the influenza epidemic of 1918. His wife and co-worker Mina, a sister of the philosopher Henri Bergson, returned to England and carried on the Order's work until her own death in 1928.

From whence did MacGregor Mathers get his knowledge? Well, he cast his net wide, and there is a rich European occult tradition to draw from. He was, in a sense, a hunter and gatherer, melding into a more or less coherent system that which was much neglected and scattered from the fields of Rosicrucianism, Freemasonry, Alchemy, Astrology, the Angelic Tablets of Dr John Dee and much else besides.

He was however much impressed and influenced by Anna Kingsford. Indeed it is to her and her co-worker Edward Maitland that he dedicated his book *The Kabballah Unveiled*. This is an English translation of the Latin *Kabbalah Denudata* of Knorr von Rosenroth. Personally I have to say that I find the title singularly inappropriate – for the book unveils very little of the Qabalah to me. Possibly it is just me that is too obtuse. I will simply say that as a user-friendly text it is a long way from Dion Fortune.

Anna Kingsford seems somewhat forgotten these days but she was undoubtedly a very remarkable and charismatic figure in her time. She was a vegetarian on moral grounds and a militant anti-vivisectionist. In this cause she went so far as to obtain a medical degree the better to fight the scientific establishment upon their own ground. This was rendered doubly difficult because the London medical schools did not admit women. Undeterred, she went to Paris, and studied and qualified as a doctor there. This was not easy for her because of her striking physical beauty, which meant she was despised by fellow women students, and constantly being propositioned by the male ones.

Her refusal to have anything to do with any experiments upon living creatures caused considerable difficulties with the teaching establishment, which considered some aspects of medicine could only be studied by such means. Nonetheless she eventually qualified, and all this despite most appalling ill health, including asthmatic attacks and intermittent black-outs associated with powerful mystical visions.

It is amazing that she achieved what she did. A spirit as passionately committed as hers, it seems, would rapidly burn out its physical vehicle. Born in 1846, she died in 1888 at the age of 42. During that time she had married an Anglican vicar, given birth to a daughter, written stories for the *Penny Post,* been received into the Roman Catholic church by Cardinal Manning, founded the Hermetic Society, become a doctor of medicine, bought and edited a magazine *The Lady's Own Paper* to combat vivisection, promoted higher education for woman, become President of the London Lodge of the Theosophical Society in England, and had a variety of mystical visions.

These were subsequently collected and published post-humously as *Clothed with the Sun.* As a Qabalist and occultist, together with her devoted collaborator Edward Maitland, she gave a series of lectures in 1881, subsequently published under the title of *The Perfect Way.* This work is specifically acknowledged by MacGregor Mathers in the dedication of his *Kabballah Unveiled.*

The Perfect Way thus made a considerable impression in its day. In brief, it taught that man is a fourfold being, consisting of spirit, body, and elements of higher and lower consciousness in between. In effect corresponding to the Four Worlds of the Qabalists – Atziluth, the Spiritual World; Briah the Creative World; Yetzirah the Formative World; and Assiah the Mundane World. Upon the same pattern was the Universe created and all knowledge of higher things could be obtained by looking within, rather than looking without to received religious dogma. Nonetheless, through the inspiration of her visions, Anna Kingsford embraced much of the iconography of the Roman Catholic church, and the whole of the Bible from Genesis through to Revelations, but interpreted it in her own way. Thus Adam and Eve signified the male and female principles of the human being, the one biased to intellect and sensation, the other to intuition and feeling, and the whole story of the Fall was a process of getting the priorities wrong between the relative importance of spirit and matter. All animal sacrifice of course she condemned as ignorant priestcraft, as well as church teachings that depended upon dogma based upon alleged historical events such as the crucifixion of Jesus as a vicarious atonement. The woman clothed with the Sun in the Revelations of St John was the triumphant feminine principle of spiritual consciousness. There is a great deal within Anna Kingsford that would strike a cord with feminist and animal rights sentiments of today.

In her own day there was considerable interest in the way that she and Helena Petrovna Blavatsky had come up with a similar type of teaching independently, the one drawing from the wisdom of the east and the other from the wisdom of the west. I think that the spirit of the times called for it. When the pupil is ready the teachers will arrive.

The Perfect Way was claimed by its authors to be no less than "a recovery of ... the basic and secret doctrine of all the religions of antiquity, including Christianity – the doctrine commonly called the Gnosis, and variously entitled Hermetic and Kabbalistic."

It was welcomed by the contemporary Qabalistic scholar Christian Guinsberg, and was accorded a particularly fulsome

93

welcome by Baron Spedalieri, a friend, disciple and literary heir of Eliphas Levi, who wrote to say that within it "we find all that there is of truth in the Kabbala, supplemented by new intuitions, such as present a body of doctrine at once complete, homogeneous, logical, and inexpugnable." He saw it moreover as a fulfilment of the prophecy of Guillaume Postel and other Hermetists of the later middle ages that the sacred books of the Hebrews should become known and understood at the end of the era. In *The Perfect Way* he thought that prophecy was accomplished.

Through Anna Kingsford we have an important link with an influential continental source, namely the Abbé Alphonse Louis Constant, who taught occultism and Qabalah under the name of Eliphas Levi. His system of correspondences between Qabalistic and occult symbolism, *Dogme et Rituel de la Haute Magie* of 1855, had been studied by Anna Kingsford when she was in Paris.

Eliphas Levi's ideas had an influence upon both sides of the English Channel. His system was taken up by French occultists under the leadership of Dr. Gerard Encausse, who wrote under the name of Papus and re-founded a version of the Martinist Order.

In England, Eliphas Levi's lead was taken up by MacGregor Mathers, and somewhat reworked to produce a different system of correspondences. Therefore to this day, if you approach an English speaking or a Francophone Qabalistic occultist you will find that they have a different set of symbolic attributions on which to base their Qabalistic exegesis, but this is not so grave a matter in practical terms as might be thought.

A biographer of Dion Fortune, Alan Richardson, has drawn a comparison between the work of Dion Fortune and Anna Kingsford. But although they may, each in their way, have made Qabalah more accessible to their contemporaries, they were very different types of women, and their initial approach to the subject was very different.

Anna Kingsford was very much a religious enthusiast who took on scientific study as a means to formalise her mystical insights, Dion Fortune however was a much more down to earth and secular kind of person who came to the religious side of her subject almost reluctantly.

She came to occultism and the Qabalah through a personal involvement with psychoanalysis. We are talking now of the era immediately before the 1st World War, when Freud's theories of the subconscious were still very much a novelty.

She gained acceptance as a lay analyst, working at a psychotherapeutic clinic, and gave some lectures, later published in book form as *The Machinery of the Mind,* with a foreword by a Fellow of the Royal Society

In the course of her work in this field however, she came to the conclusion that although the psychoanalytic approach had its merits, it did not go nearly far enough. There were a number of things which she felt could only be adequately explained by recourse to occult traditions. In this she was, in some respects, anticipating Jungian psychology. However, although Jung has quarried widely within the occult traditions he has nonetheless remained outside them, as a psychotherapist. Dion Fortune however, went the whole hog and founded an occult school.

To a certain extent she may have been pushed into this when psychiatry became the prerogative of the formally medically qualified, and the nearest that Dion Fortune ever got to the British Medical Association was to marry a doctor, Dr. Thomas Penry Evans. The two of them together undertook some interesting research into esoteric therapeutics, most of which was only ever shown to qualified practitioners who had occult interests, not a very numerous species I have to say. At long last however much of this material is now published as *Principles of Esoteric Healing*. [Sun Chalice, 2000].

How did Dion Fortune, as an occultist with a psychoanalytical background, see the Qabalah? In many respects largely as a universal compendium or even filing cabinet. This is how she refers to the Tree of Life at the beginning of *The Mystical Qabalah:* "The curious symbol system known to us as the Tree of Life is an attempt to reduce to diagrammatic form every force and factor in the manifested universe and the soul of man....In brief, the Tree of Life is a compendium of science, psychology, philosophy and theology."

A compendium of science, psychology, philosophy and theology. That is a pretty tall order. But I think she was choosing her words with care. For those four categories neatly summarise in plain terms the four levels of understanding by which the Tree of Life can be approached. They are sometimes referred to as the Four Worlds of the Qabalists. That is to say:

what she meant by science was Assiah, the Material World;
what she meant by psychology was Yetzirah, the Formative World;
what she meant by philosophy was Briah, the CreativeWorld;
and by theology she meant Atziluth, the Spiritual or Archetypal World.

Now when we speak of science, psychology, philosophy and theology in this context we are taking a somewhat different approach to them than might be assumed in the outer world. Her assumptions are firmly neo-platonist. This is clearly implied when she says that in the Tree of Life is to be found every force and factor (a) in the manifested universe and (b) in the soul of man.

That is to say, understand the universe and you understand the soul. Understand the soul and you understand the universe. This is the Hermetic axiom "As above – so below". The microcosm, which is man, is a reflection of the Macrocosm, which is the universe – each having been created in the image and likeness of God. For the Qabalistic occultist, the Tree of Life is a divinely inspired framework or pattern of the soul of man and of the universe. There are of course other frameworks that are available. For different cultures the revelation has been different, but the underlying reality they represent remains the same.

Dion Fortune looked upon the Tree of Life as a fundamental part of what she liked to call the Western Esoteric Tradition, as compared say to the chakra systems of the Eastern Esoteric Tradition. Indeed she often referred to the Qabalah as the yoga of the west.

It is possible to cross-reference one system against another. The detailed correspondences will not be exact, but the general plan is the same, for it is the same inner framework of interior reality that is being represented. The Thousand Petaled Sahasrara Chakra above the head, has its parallel in the Sephirah Kether, the Fount of Creation. The Four Petaled Muladhara Chakra at the base of the spine has its parallel with the Sephirah Malkuth, the Sphere of the Four Elements.

These polar points in the subtle body correspond to the polar points of the spiritual divine spark and the physical vehicle we inhabit. There is, however a vast area in between, consisting of different levels and modes of consciousness – that may be referred to in their objective aspect by various terms – the soul of the world, the anima mundi, the astral light, even the collective unconscious.

This field of consciousness is exceedingly diverse and complex. It is a great sea of tides and influences and ever changing Protean forms. In simple terms it might be envisaged as an energy field that exists between two magnetic poles. One cosmic or spiritual; and the other physical or elemental. As far as the Qabalistic occultist is concerned, that complex field of consciousness can best be approached and described in terms of the structures of the Tree of Life.

Now it seems to me that the original Jewish Qabalists, those God intoxicated men, left us with a very simple framework. But having inherited that very simple framework, for better or for worse, we modern occultists, from Eliphas Levi onwards, have been very busy complicating it.

It is as if we have been left a great Temple by our rabbinical forebears. A Temple of such holiness that there is no image within it. Simply various rooms, all of them empty, but for the Divine Presence, in one of its emanations or another.

If we go into a particular room, and quietly chant a particular sound, the Name of God that forms the Word of Power within that particular sacred space, that Sephirah, then we may experience a particular revelation of God to the soul. Or we may perhaps allow ourselves to invoke a particular Archangel or representative of an Angelic Choir that is assigned to each particular divine space. That is about the sum of it.

However, what do we find when the occultists take over? Not content with empty rooms of divine immanence, we bring in lots of furniture, symbolic chairs, sofas, divans, pictures on the walls, potted plants, listed correspondences of every conceivable nature. Fortunately, behind all this *bric a brac* the divine presence remains, even though it sometimes appears to be forgotten.

There are also of course all the corridors between these holy chambers; that are traditionally known as the Mystical Paths of Concealed Glory. Each may have been reverently designated by a particular letter from the Word of God. But thanks to the firms of symbolic furniture emporia, founding proprietors Levi and Mathers, they are now duly fitted out with pictures from the Tarot Trumps and an assortment of astrological signs and symbols together with selections from the various pantheons of pagan gods.

From this perspective I can quite see why Professor Scholem, in his seminal work *Major Trends in Jewish Mysticism* was moved to dismiss the works of many Qabalistic occultists as "highly coloured nonsense". I am sure that, to anyone who regards the Qabalah as a hallowed ground of colloquy with the God of their Fathers, this Gentile occult invasion must seem not only nonsensical, but probably blasphemous, sinister and rather seedy as well.

However, in the face of such possible strictures, I can only make due apology to any whose religious sensibilities we may have offended, and after my forty five years of experience of shifting symbolic furniture around say, rather after the fashion of Galileo: – "Yes – I know it may not fit well with your religious perspectives. I know that this whole procedure may well seem bizarre or even crazy – but – nonetheless - it works!"

But we have to learn to forge a language capable of comprehending and communicating truths that may very often only be expressed in terms of paradox. There are two principle means of communication that lie at our disposal – one in terms of pictures, the other in terms of words.

In an occult context, the pictures will be a system of evocative symbols. The words are likely to be in the form of messages, often of an inspirational power that exceeds their surface prosaic meaning, and which may indeed sometimes seem to be obscure or couched in language that is poetic or even mantic.

Let us take two specific examples – in the one case – tarot cards. In the other case - the Qabalistic tradition of the meggid. Both examples, as it happens, have connections with Oxford.

In the matter of Tarot cards, I call to mind a labour of love by an Oxford don, Professor Michael Dummet, who happened to have a perennial interest in card games and their history. This led him also to a study of the game of Tarot, where he suddenly found himself standing at the top of a slippery slope which leads down into the abyss of occult applications of the Tarot. As a Professor of Logic I think it fair to say, from my reading of his book *The Game of Tarot,* that the further he got into this, the more horrified he became.

It seemed as if a slough of irrationality threatened to engulf him. In his first book he simply gave up the attempt to make any sense of modern esoteric theory and practice but, after enlisting the help of some colleagues, he followed up with a

book called *A Wicked Pack of Cards* on the origins of the occult
Tarot in the 19th century, in collaboration with two specialist
historians, Ronald Decker and Thierry Depaulis, and I gather
is even considering a sequel to deal with some 20th century
developments. I am all for this kind of academic research into
aspects of the occult world, even if it usually seems to be
reserved to the spheres of history or anthropology. I only ask
that the history is accurate, and I have to say that I have come
across some appalling slipshod scholarship on the part of history
dons who ought to know better. I also wish I had a pound for
every piece of advice I have given to anthropology students
writing a thesis for their Ph.D. In some respects I find that I am
in the odd position of being a primary source. Indeed I am
wondering if I should not try to find a soft option in some
liberal religious studies faculty, who might accept my doing an
M.A. on "The Works of Gareth Knight."

Unfortunately some less experienced occult students do feel
threatened by academic research such as this, rather after the
fashion that a fundamentalist Christian might feel attacked
or betrayed by academic Biblical criticism. After all a good
deal of occultism, as indeed of religion, depends upon faith in
a particular tradition. If you believe in something then you
make the conditions necessary for the noumenous to work.
Someone desecrating your altars with facts is therefore not
necessarily very welcome, or indeed very useful.

A certain Oxford alumnus of the 19th century seemed to
understand this. I don't know whether Lewis Carroll was a
closet occultist or Qabalist but he spoke some profound
wisdom at times. I am thinking of the bellman in *The Hunting
of the Snark* when he took some people on a mysterious voyage.
Let us assume that the Snark is some higher vision or wisdom.
As they disembarked he seized each one by the piece of hair

close to their Sahasrara Chakra and proclaimed:

> "Just the place for a Snark!" the Bellman cried,
>   As he landed his crew with care,
> Supporting each man at the top of the tide
>   By a finger entwined in his hair.

> "Just the place for a Snark! I have said it twice:
>   That alone should encourage the crew.
> Just the place for a Snark! I have said it thrice:
>   What I tell you three times is true."

This is the kind of paradoxical truth in occultism that has its equivalent in the mind experiment of Schrodinger's cat in sub-atomic physics. And if either statement does not profoundly shock you then you have not grasped the full force of their truth. They subvert our natural ideas of reality in the material world about us. Of course what the anti-vivisectionist Anna Kingsford might have thought of the experiment on Schrodingers cat, is something yet again.

Anyhow, despite their eminently common sense point of view I felt that Michael Dummet and his friends had rather jumped to the conclusion that because we occultists believe a set of assumptions that turn out to be historically untrue, we have been deliberately set on fooling ourselves or misleading an unsuspecting public.

The point is that as a working occultist I have found the images of the Tarot to be an extremely useful appendage to Qabalistic studies. It seemed from this fact of experience, to be a reasonable assumption that, in the neoplatonic circles of Renaissance Italy, they had been specifically designed for just that. Indeed specimens of the earliest cards I have seen, encrusted with gold leaf, seem to me more suited to meditation or even ritual purposes than playing vulgar card games.

However, as Professor Dummet has established, the earliest packs vary, not only in design but in the number of cards they contain, and the original Trumps bear no names or numbers. Only when they became printed from wood blocks for use by the hoi poloi were they invested with numbers and names. Also, their numerical order varied from one region to another and the version that has come down to us today, as the Marseilles Tarot, is not so much the result of a body of hidden masters designing a secret number system, but rather evolving through commercial and historical accident, because Marseilles had the most successful card printing and distribution industry.

Mundane factors such as these form the basis upon which nineteenth century occultists derived their esoteric systems, which have been accepted as ancient wisdom by their twentieth century successors.

Of course it could be said that this makes the Tarot system even more wondrous, for it virtually designed itself. However, be this as it may, from my own lifetime of studying occultists at work, my view is that one system of symbolic attributes will work as well as another, if you are prepared to invest enough faith and sincerity into it.

It is for this reason that beginners are advised to stick to one system and forget about all others. This may seem a blinkered and sectarian view but it does avoid getting into a speculative intellectual muddle, like the starving donkey between two bales of hay which could not make its mind up.

What the Tarot is, therefore, is not so much a closed system of arcane secrets, as a selection from a treasure house of stock images in the public domain of the collective human psyche. Some of these images naturally turn up even in ancient Egyptian hieroglyphic art but that does not mean that the system as we know it was invented at the time of the Pharoahs.

What we are concerned with, in applying pictorial symbolic systems such as the Tarot to the Tree of Life in various ways, is a technology of the imagination. And here is I speak of the imagination in Coleridgean terms. That is to say, of the creative powers of the human mind rather than the arbitrary fancy. For the imagination has a profound internal structure, and this is what makes the Tree of Life such a valuable device to the occultist.

Try to conceive consciousness as being like a very concentrated solution of a crystalline salt. If you pass that solution beyond a certain point of concentration it will suddenly completely crystallise. What is important about the Qabalah, is that the lines of crystalline structure within the imagination will take up the alignments and inter-relationships of the glyph of the Tree of Life.

So there you have another line upon the principles of *Solve* and *Coagule* of the alchemists.

The Qabalistic Tree of Life is the pattern for the underlying structure of what has been variously called the collective unconscious, or the astral light, or the anima mundi – all the terms are no better than suggestive - indeed in many respects inadequate – but I trust you may intuitively know what I mean.

104

We are engaged in mapping the bottom of a great sea, a great lake of consciousness, between Kether and Malkuth, from which faery ladies bearing magic swords may come, messengers and delegates from great submarine worlds in another dimension of reality.

But enough of pictorial imagery. Let us turn to the other approach to these matters through the medium of inspired words.

An interesting example of this form of practical Qabalah is to be found in a work of Owen Barfield, another Oxford man, and also a Coleridge expert as it happens. He was one of the famous group of Oxford friends known as the Inklings, that included C.S.Lewis, Charles Williams and Tolkien. Barfield hardly regarded himself as a Qabalist. He leaned more to the teachings of another great occultist, Rudolf Steiner, who in turn derived much of his inspiration from Goethe.

In his book *Unancestral Voice,* [published in 1965 by, of all the unlikely sounding publishers of such material, the Wesleyan University Press] Owen Barfield gives an account, which I think must surely be autobiographical, of a contact with a kind of Qabalistic intelligence.

He cites as an authority the work of a 16th century Jewish rabbi, Joseph Karo, who, like Barfield, was a lawyer, and one deeply interested in the spiritual side of life. He kept a diary known as the *Maggid Mesharim,* and in this he recorded details of communication with a kind of inner voice that spoke within his mind in periods of silence and solitude. However, as some of his contemporaries bore witness, it was sometimes known to inspire Karo to speak its words aloud and spontaneously.

Karo and his friends tried to identify this inner voice with various possible sources. As an angel. As the spirit of that record of traditional teachings known as the Mishnah. Or even as the Shekinah, the presence of God in Malkuth. Had they been contemporaries of ours they might also I suppose have added a variety of other theories, ranging from New Age channelling to clinical schizophrenia.

The protagonist of Barfield's account, decides however to cast aside all modern prejudices and try out contacting a meggid for himself. And he finds, as a result of his Qabalistic meditations, that realisations are coming into his mind in answer to specific questions.

In the course of time this develops into a more objective state when he discovers that he is becoming a voluntary mouthpiece for what appears to be a superior intelligence. He finds himself uttering, with all the confidence of personal experience, things that he could not possibly have known from personal experience. This comprised the second stage of his contact with the meggid.

The third stage was even more surprising. It occurred at a scientific conference, where our hero decides to invoke the presence of the meggid, on the off-chance that this might inspire him to contribute to the debate. He becomes aware of the approach of the meggid through what he calls "a variety of subtle psychosomatic indicators." He does not say what these were but I imagine he refers to the itch of the pineal gland at the brow or a vague sense of pins and needles around the cranium, which are fairly common indicators of higher consciousness awakening.

However, when the meggid arrives, it completely ignores his own somewhat limited brain consciousness, and appears to go straight to one of the speakers, who seems suddenly inspired. He gives his critics more than they bargained for and the whole discussion winds up in his favour. What is more remarkable in all of this however, is that the meggid, which up to now had appeared to have merely a subjective existence, has taken on an objective status – in its ability to contact the minds of others.

Our hero thus thinks he had better begin to address the meggid, not in terms of an archetypal image from his own subconscious, but in time honoured style as "Master". Only to be gently reminded by the meggid that it regards itself as his servant. And to the degree that he renders service to others.

This brings us back to the religious and ethical dynamic which seems to me fundamental in any practical study of occultism or of Qabalah.

For me, this attitude is expressed in its fullness in the 17th century, which in many ways might be regarded as the fountainhead of the modern tradition. It saw the circulation of the Rosicrucian documents at its commencement, the spirit of which I think is the essence of Qabalistic occultism.

Actually, almost all 17th century writings and diagrams appear somewhat occult to us because of the spirit of the times, when the old religious approach to the universe was giving place to the scientific method – and the two were still somewhat in balance. The secular had not squeezed the life out of the spiritual view of man and the universe. Johannes Kepler, for example, who discovered the mathematical formula for the motions of the planets was still sufficiently influenced by Pythagorean mysticism to spend a very considerable effort in trying to interpret them in terms of the Platonic solids. The great mathematician Newton was deep in alchemical experiments.

Athanasius Kircher seems a typical representative of the 17th century, and looks to us even more esoteric than he was because of his research into ancient civilisations.

In his most famous book *Oedipus Egypticus* he pursued the theory that all religions are derived from one, that of Ancient Egypt. He analyses the cults of Zoroaster, the Orphic Hymns, the Golden Verses of Pythagoras, the Chaldean Oracles, the works of Plato, and of the Neoplatonists Iambliuchus, Plotinus and Proclus, the Chaldean Oracles, as well as the Qabalah, and sees them all as derivatives from Ancient Egypt.

How is this possible, we may ask ourselves, from a Jesuit, not only living in Rome, where Giordano Bruno had been burned at the stake a generation before, but officially recognised as an academic authority by the Roman Catholic church?

It was because he set all of these ancient belief systems forth as being but primitive foreshadowings of the true religion revealed by his own church. Nonetheless, to modern eyes, it would require only a slight change of emphasis from regarding all religions as having a common origin, to their being offshoots or interpretations, or even misunderstandings, of a universal perennial philosophy. Anyhow, Kircher went very close to saying this, without ending up the way that other enthusiasts of ancient wisdom did. Or perhaps it is not what you say it's the way that you say it, that keeps you out of hot water.

An immediate forerunner of his, better represents the best in the Christian tradition of the Qabalah, the author of *The Mosaical Philosophy* – Robert Fludd. He was another Oxford graduate. He graduated Bachelor of Arts at this University, in 1596, with a thesis on music. And after obtaining his Master's degree in 1598 left on a six year tour of France, Spain, Italy and Germany, during which he discovered a vocation for medicine. He returned to Oxford in 1605 to study medicine and after one or two brushes with medical orthodoxy eventually set up in medical practice in Fenchurch Street, London at the age of 35.

He also devoted himself to writing great encyclopedic works such as the *History of the Macrocosm.* In these he pursues a philosophy that combines practical examination of nature with a spiritual view of the universe, as an intelligent hierarchy of conscious beings; and the proper end of men to be the direct knowledge of God.

Although he wrote in Latin, interest in his works has been sustained because of his gift for casting his philosophy into diagrammatic form, and some of Fludd's diagrams, such as the famous Anima Mundi, remain most evocative adjuncts to a study of the Qabalah.

Nor to him was a Rosicrucian rubric such as "Under the shadow of thy wings Jehovah" a quaint pious formula, it was a reality of faith. Just as he could represent the creation coming out of the Ain Soph by the dove of the Holy Spirit sweeping in a grand circle over the Waters of Primal Chaos.

As a former student of music, fundamental to his beliefs was the idea of a harmonious relationship between man as a miniature universe, and the universe as a great living organism, both of them cast in the image of their divine Creator. He expressed this often in terms of musical harmony, derived from Pythagorean and Platonic number theory.

As an Anglican Protestant he had a broader and more tolerent base than his younger contemporary the Jesuit Athanasius Kircher.

We may have lost some of the piety of these earlier occultists and Qabalists in our own day, and if so I think we are the poorer for it. It was an ideal that still pertained at the beginning of the 19th century, even in someone like Francis Barrett in *The Magus,* published in 1801, which is in many respects a popularisation of more ancient work.

What he asks of the reader I will state to you. "Thou art a man in whose soul the image of Divinity is sealed for eternity. Think first, what is thy desire in searching after these mysteries? Is it wealth, honour, fame, power, might, aggrandisement, and the like?

"Perhaps thy heart says, All these would I gladly crave!"

"If so, this is my answer – seek first to know thyself thoroughly, cleanse thy heart from all wicked, vain and rapacious desires. To know thyself is to know God, for it is the spiritual gift from God that enables a man to know himself. This gift but very few possess as may be daily seen."

"Seek ye first the kingdom of God, and all things shall be added unto you."

"Farewell, remember my poor counsel, and be happy."

8
ANNA KINGSFORD –
THE PASSIONATE PIONEER

Anna Kingsford with her concern for animal rights and the equality of women would not seem out of place in the modern world, yet she was born in the early Victorian period, in 1846.

She was also naturally clairvoyant and subject to a mystical visionary facility either in sleep or in trance, although she preferred to think of this in terms of prophecy, in the Biblical sense. It led to her becoming a pioneer of the revival of the Mystery Tradition before either the Theosophical Society or the Hermetic Order of the Golden Dawn had become established in England. Indeed she played a significant part in the initial formation of both, and it was a matter of some surprise that she foreshadowed much Theosophical teaching independently from her own interior vision, to say nothing of her pioneering work on the Qabalah and the Greek and Egyptian Mysteries that later played a major role in Golden Dawn knowledge papers and rituals.

There are certain parallels between her own life and that of Dion Fortune, as has been tentatively suggested in some circles in the past. Both were imaginative children who had early literary work published; both had the protection of an older man to act as adviser, collaborator and general factotum; both developed powers of inner vision and communication, both researched western esoteric sources, embraced esoteric Christianity, and were pioneers of presenting Qabalistic teaching in accessible form; both had medical interests and connections; both had a concern for animal welfare and vegetarianism (although Dion Fortune's attitude was more pragmatic as compared to Anna Kingsford's uncompromising stance); both were initially thought to have died immediately after being born. However, although a gap of two years between the death of Anna Kingsford and the birth of Dion Fortune makes reincarnation technically possible, a more likely connection is that they came into the world as initiates with similar abilities and a common destiny. Furthermore, just as Dion Fortune's close colleagues felt post mortem contacts with her to attend to unfinished business, so are similar contacts recorded with Anna Kingsford until at least 1893, which, if true, rather precludes an 1890 reincarnation as Dion Fortune!

Anna had a somewhat lonely childhood. Although the youngest of twelve children to a London merchant and ship owner, John Bonus, there was a long gap between her and her next oldest sibling. She was extremely imaginative and not only believed in fairies but identified with them. So much so that she had to be forcibly removed from a pantomime performance when she tried to join the fairies on stage, regarding them as her own people.

Learning that trying to speak of her visionary experiences only led to her being taken to the doctor with resultant doses of physic or worse, (such as having all her hair cut off), she diverted her imagination into writing stories and poems. Much of her juvenile verse was published in various magazines and a long story *Beatrice: a Tale of the Early Christians,* written at the age of thirteen, so impressed the editor of the *Churchman's Companion* magazine that he published it as a book, and also a volume of her poems under the title *River Reeds*.

Her formal education was much interrupted by illness as she was a delicate child but concluded with attendance at a fashionable Brighton finishing school, where she came under a cloud for having too independent a mind on religious subjects. When she rejoined her family she continued writing historical and fantasy stories for magazines, some of which were later published in volume form as *Rosamunda the Princess* and *Dreams and Dream Stories.*

She seems at this time to have been a pretty outgoing head-strong sort of girl, for she loved riding, and when her health permitted might well spend all day in the saddle. This included riding to hounds, which caused her no moral problems at first, even when being in at the kill, until one day she experienced a sudden revulsion from it all and dedicated the rest of her life to animal welfare, becoming a pioneer vegetarian and dauntless campaigner against vivisection. Indeed if she is remembered today it is more in the role of a pioneer vegetarian and animal rights campaigner than as occultist.

The death of her father in 1865, to whom she had been much attached, was a major event in her teen-age life but at least it made her financially independent. This was just as well, for there was strong family pressure for her to marry a wealthy but elderly suitor. She preferred a love match with her cousin, Algernon Godfrey Kingsford, who had leanings towards the church. Eventually she got her way, although not until she had legally come of age, and the two were married on the last day of 1867.

A few weeks before her marriage she had been introduced to spiritualism by a local woman, and apparently received a contact from her father. It was not long before she found that she could make contacts readily for herself and she continued to pursue spiritualistic experiments whilst living in Lichfield, where her husband was in the process of taking holy orders in the Church of England.

Hers were by no means in the ordinary run of spiritualist contacts however, for they included one with King Henry VIII's second wife, Anne Boleyn, by automatic writing, in January 1869. An interesting element of this is that when writing up an account of this, her biographer Edward Maitland made excuses for the fact that the spirit of Anne Boleyn referred to having her head cut off with a sword, when of course, he said, what was really meant must have been an axe. However, in point of fact, Anne Boleyn was, by her special request, executed by a swordsman, brought over from France for the occasion.

Later she identified strongly with Anne Boleyn, as well as Joan or Arc and Mary Magdalen, and whether or not there was any reincarnationary link, as she liked to think, there was no doubt she bore a certain archetypal resemblance in various ways to these remarkable women. She was certainly as pugnacious and visionary a campaigner as Joan of Arc, and she was inclined to account for her physical ills as expiation for leaping ambition and sins of the flesh in the past.

Anna gave birth to a daughter within a year of her marriage although it was to be her only child, nor did she have a great deal to do with the girl's up-bringing, despite her pronounced views on child education. A combination of her delicate health and extensive peripatetic activities also meant that she and her husband lived more as brother and sister than husband and wife for the rest of their lives together. It proved a perplexing burden for Anna that she seemed destined to be a wife and yet no wife, a mother and yet no mother as a result of her bouts of ill health and ceaseless campaigning.

She demonstrated a further independence of mind in being received into the Roman Catholic church in September 1870. She took the baptismal name of Mary Magdalen and was confirmed by Cardinal Manning two years later, with the additional names of Maria Johanna. It would appear, however, that although attracted to the religious symbolism of the Roman Catholic tradition, she had little time for orthodox dogma or for actual church attendance.

Meanwhile her husband was appointed curate at Atcham, near Shrewsbury, where he eventually became vicar. Apart from her spiritualist contacts and Roman Catholic affiliation it was obvious that Anna was not going to be any ordinary Anglican vicar's wife. A national magazine, *The Lady's Own Paper: a Journal of Progress, Taste and Art,* came up for sale, which she purchased, editing the magazine herself, and commuting between London and Shrewsbury in order to do so. She used the magazine as a campaigning platform against vivisection and in favour of a vegetarian dietary regime. However, so uncompromising were her views that she refused a great deal of advertising upon ethical grounds, and so the project eventually became insolvent.

In the Spring of 1873 she decided that she needed to fight vivisection from within the enemy camp by becoming qualified as a medical doctor. At this time however no medical school in England would accept women as students. Nothing loath, she decided to study in Paris. This raised considerable logistical problems, for her husband was unable to accompany her, and her health was delicate enough to cause concern about her trying to live in Paris alone. Here it seems that fate lent a hand for she met up with Edward Maitland.

Maitland was some twenty two years her senior, a widower, who had led an adventurous life as a "forty-niner" in the Californian gold rush, and had then gone on to Australia for some years before returning to England with his young son, to help look after his aged mother. A giant of a man physically, he was a gentle introverted soul with mystical, historical and literary interests. Upon reading a novel of his, Anna Kingsford wrote him a letter of appreciation, which led to their meeting, where they struck up an immediate accord, almost one of mutual recognition.

It so happened that Maitland had some free time available, and so with the concurrence and even to the relief of her husband, Maitland agreed to accompany Anna on her first visit to Paris. This developed into something of a regular arrangement during the college terms. They passed as uncle and niece to still wagging Parisian tongues, and sometimes her husband or her mother stood in when Maitland was not available.

Anna had by no means an easy time in France. She was a young woman of striking beauty and considerable charisma, tall and of clear complexion with a mass of golden hair. As a result most of her women fellow students despised her, whilst their male colleagues tried to proposition her. Indeed she found it virtually impossible to walk alone through Parisian streets without being molested in some way or another; contemporary Frenchmen considering a beautiful lone female at once an invitation and a challenge.

Her main tutor also took an instant prejudice against her, to the point of victimisation, assuming by some strange logic that a beautiful woman who wanted to become a doctor must be some kind of sexual deviant or freak of nature. This was only relieved when he discovered that she had considerable artistic ability and was able to make accurate drawings of some surgical appliances that he had invented. After that, her path became a little easier.

Nonetheless, the whole course of her medical studies was tormented by the general attitude towards experimentation upon live animals, which she refused to countenance, although attitudes toward treating pauper patients were little better, who might well be painfully used as demonstration material for students. "C'est pour la science!" was the matter of fact and somewhat surprised response to her when she protested against such practices. She obtained some relief by gaining permission to pursue some of her studies in London under private tuition. Although even here she found herself obliged to dismiss certain tutors who insisted that physiology could only be learned by personally replicating experiments upon living creatures. This she resolutely refused to do.

In the end, despite all these difficulties over six years of study, she gained her qualification as doctor of medicine in 1880. Her doctoral dissertation, *L'Alimentation Végétale de l'Homme,* upon the thesis that human beings were naturally vegetarians, was later published in English as *The Perfect Way in Diet.* She practiced medicine in London, with particular emphasis on women patients, and was also now able to use her medical prestige and knowledge as ammunition on her anti-vivisection lecture campaigns.

During the whole of this time she had continued to have visions, or what she called "illuminations". These occurred sometimes in sleep as vivid dreams, sometimes in trance, either voluntarily induced or coming suddenly upon her so that she was struck down in a state of collapse.

The results of these visions, recorded by herself or Edward Maitland, led them to believe that they had a special mission, apart from animal welfare concerns, to teach an esoteric interpretation of Christianity. They supplemented her illuminations with research into the mystery religions of Greece and Egypt and the works of other western visionaries such as Emanuel Swedenborg and Jacob Boehme. Anna had a high regard for their visions, although she considered that some were of less worth than others and could be distorted by their not being vegetarians. Like Blavatsky's mahatmas, she insisted that total abstinence from alcohol and meat eating was essential for purity of vision.

In the summer of 1881 they decided to give a series of private lectures to an invited audience in London, which were so well received that they were published as a book early the next year, at first anonymously, under the title *The Perfect Way*.

Their general thesis was that all religions, from ancient pagan times to modern Christianity, have the same symbolic message behind them. In the case of Christianity, it was particularly necessary to interpret Old and New Testament stories not simply in terms of historical events, open to argument and dispute, but as personal spiritual experience.

The alternative title to *The Perfect Way* was *The Finding of Christ*, that is to say the Christ within, or the spark of eternal spirit within the human soul. They used the term Soul to mean the unit of higher consciousness surrounding the spirit, that reincarnates in a series of physical bodies and personalities, or what in later popular Theosophical Society teaching was known as the Higher Self.

Anna, with her medical background, was fond of using the model of a living cell to describe this. The cell is basically a four-fold structure, that has an outer membrane, (which corresponds to the human body), containing protoplasm, (which corresponds to the thoughts and feelings and general experience of the personality). Inside this is an inner core or nucleolus, (which corresponds to the reincarnating Soul), and at the heart of the cell a nucleus, (corresponding to the immortal spirit).

An alternative more homely analogy could be the egg, with its shell, white, yolk, and germ of life. Another could be an ancient lamp, with the clay body, the oil, the wick and the flame. The same four divisions could be found in the external world, as the physical universe, the astral world, the angelic or soul world, and the presence of God.

Much of this should have a familiar ring to students of *The Cosmic Doctrine* and it also accords with the Qabalistic diagram of the Tree of Life. The Supernal Triangle with its cosmic background corresponding to the Spirit; the higher triangle of Chesed, Geburah and Tiphareth corresponding to the Higher Self and World of Souls; the lower triangle of Netzach, Hod and Yesod to the astral realms; and Malkuth to the physical world.

The Perfect Way made an enormous impression upon contemporary London society and MacGregor Mathers, not usually one to praise another's work, described it as "one of the most deeply occult works that has been written for centuries" and confirmed its compatibility with the Qabalah. This view was fulsomely endorsed by others, including Baron Spedalieri, the personal student and inheritor of the works of the famous French occultist Eliphas Levi.

Baron Spedalieri went so far as to claim that *The Perfect Way* completely surpassed all previous Qabalistic exegesis. Whilst Jewish students of the Qabalah might dispute this, in view of their own diverse, extensive and subtle literature, it was nonetheless true enough in terms of accessible texts for a gentile audience. There was probably nothing to touch it in this respect until the popular Qabalistic works of Israel Regardie and Dion Fortune some fifty years later.

When the London branch of the Theosophical Society was founded in 1881, although Anna Kingsford was not a member, because of her prominence upon the London esoteric scene she was invited to become its first President, a post which she took up in May 1882 upon returning from an extensive continental lecture tour. She voluntarily gave up the post a year later, however, in favour of A.P.Sinnett, to whom the famous "mahatma letters" had been addressed. Now returning to England upon his retirement from being editor of an influential English language newspaper in India, as a convinced disciple of Madame Blavatsky and her masters Koot Hoomi and Morya he was a natural rallying point for those who felt similarly drawn to this eastern source of teaching.

The "mahatma letters" expounding esoteric doctrine, had been sent to him, sometimes by apparently occult means, from October 1880, and were used by him as the basis for his book *The Occult World,* published in 1881. He followed this up a little later with *Esoteric Buddhism* for the letters continued coming to him until 1884. It appears however that Sinnett's education into the mahatmas' teachings had been somewhat incomplete when he first met Anna Kingsford, for whilst she embraced the doctrine of reincarnation, he was still unaware of it, and indeed denied it until later receiving confirmation of it from his eastern teachers. It is worth mentioning this, not as a debating point in an ancient controversy, but as a rebuttal of the common assumption that reincarnation is a doctrine that has its origin solely in the east.

Whilst Sinnett and many other members of the Theosophical Society put great store upon Madame Blavatsky's "mahatmas", Anna Kingsford declined to give unquestioning allegiance to them. She felt that it was more important to develop one's own spiritual contacts rather than to grant authority to an unknown and remote body of men whose very existence might be called into question, whatever the claims for their super-normal powers.

Any idealistic vision of a united society dedicated to open minded discovery of universal truth behind world religions was soon impaled upon the horns of an east-west dilemma. When it became apparent that no compromise seemed likely within the London branch of the Theosophical Society as currently constituted, Anna Kingsford willingly gave up all claim to the Presidency, and although she and Maitland remained ordinary members of the Society, they decided the best way forward would be to form an independent but complementary organisation.

Thus the Hermetic Society was inaugurated in May 1884. It organised an impressive panel of lecturers, which included

S.L.MacGregor Mathers, (who later wrote *The Kabbalah Unveiled*) and Dr. Wynn Westcott, translator of the early Qabalistic text the *Sepher Yetzirah*. These two went on to become founding members of the Hermetic Order of the Golden Dawn, which might well be regarded as having risen from Anna Kingsford and Edward Maitland's vision and example. Indeed, Mathers dedicated his book to them both. It is also significant that, although the Golden Dawn derived much from a male dominated masonic tradition, it treated women as equals – and this was probably due in no small measure to Anna Kingsford's influence. The Hermetic Society came to an end with Anna Kingsford's premature death in February 1888, and the Hermetic Order of the Golden Dawn was founded a few months later.

Anna Kingsford preferred to regard herself as a mystic rather than an occultist and did not seem to be naturally inclined towards the idea of an organisation dispensing initiations. However, it was to occultism that she turned, in a most practical, and indeed controversial manner, for the furtherance of her anti-vivisection crusade.

Throughout her life she had demonstrated an extreme sensitivity to the cruelties of life, which no doubt contributed to her vulnerability to asthma, neuralgia and visionary black-outs. She was completely uncompromising in her fight against animal experimentation and to Maitland's awed admiration faced down all leaders of continental anti-vivisection movements whenever they advocated any political compromise as the best way forward, such as admitting licensed and restricted use where due cause could be admitted for the benefit of human medicine. She would accept nothing short of a complete ban.

She also tried to organise a deputation to the Pope to change the Vatican's teaching, which on the grounds that animals had no souls, declined to make any pronouncements as to their welfare. She was much depressed about the lack of sympathy with which this was received and on a trip to Italy could not bring herself to walk through the streets of Naples on account of the deplorable attitude shown toward domestic animals. In particular she was immensely distressed by the activities of a group of medical researchers in Paris, because one of them, Louis Pasteur, was regarded as an international celebrity and a national hero.

She resolved that the only way to stop these horrors was by occult means. She approached Madame Blavatsky to seek her cooperation, who, despite the strained relations at the time of the foundation of the London Lodge of the Theosophical Society, had developed a considerable respect and even affection for Anna. However, the old lady advised strongly against any such action, saying that she would only be likely to injure herself and do injury to others, without much benefiting the poor animals; that one had to work against principles, not against personalities.

Anna Kingsford would have none of this. As Edward Maitland recounts, on her receiving the letter, she exclaimed: "Attack the principles, and not the persons! And while the world is being educated to recognise the principle, millions of poor creatures are being horribly tortured, to say nothing of souls degraded and damned. I will tell you what that means. It means that whenever you see a ruffian brutally ill-treating a woman or a child, instead of rushing with all your might to the rescue, you are to stand by and do nothing but talk, or else go home and write something 'attacking the principle'. No; the power to interfere and save imposes the duty to interfere and save; and as that power has been given to me, I should not be doing my duty if I did not exercise it."

She was indeed quite capable of direct physical action when provoked, and had come home one day with a broken parasol following an altercation with the father of a boy who had been ill treating a dog. Following that incident she carried a stout stick. Certainly she now believed that as a result of private training she had received from some unknown practitioner, she possessed occult power.

A note in her diary of November 12th reveals this, after reading a press report of the death of Professor Paul Bert of the Sorbonne through a wasting-away illness. His treatment of animals was notorious, making it difficult for landlords to rent apartments within hearing distance of the cries of animals in the university laboratories, and she records that she had been wishing him to death for some months. She now felt she had proved her ability and intended to set her sights on Louis Pasteur, who was experimenting on dogs in an effort to develop a vaccine for rabies.

This was obviously no light matter, and she devoted a lengthy entry in her diary of November 17th striving to justify her actions and prove to herself that she had not fallen into the practice of black magic and the risk of bringing karmic retribution upon her head. Maitland himself, who declined to go along with her in these operations, certainly felt that this may have occurred.

Whether or not her occult operations were effective, or whether her own deep seated doubts about her integrity in this matter caused a psychosomatic reaction, there was a strange sequence of events immediately following this diary entry. That same day she went round to Pasteur's institute, ostensibly to obtain first hand evidence of what he was doing, but was unable to obtain entry, having arrived at the wrong hour. Resolving to return the next day, she was caught in a torrential shower of rain on the way home, and as a result suddenly went down with pneumonia. This rapidly deteriorated into pulmonary consumption, from which she never recovered, and she suffered a lingering illness that completely incapacitated her until her death fourteen months later at the age of forty two.

Even her deathbed was surrounded by controversy. A Roman Catholic newspaper claimed that she had made a deathbed recantation of all her work and died a good Catholic, a story bitterly contested by her husband and Edward Maitland. The story seems unlikely, in view of her strongly held opinions all her life, but was occasioned by her being attended whilst in a state of terminal weakness by a nurse who was also a devout Catholic who took it upon herself to call a priest to administer the sacraments and hear her confession. Whatever the attitude of mind of the dying woman all no doubt acted in good faith according to their lights, but the dispute lingered on with acrimony throughout all the obituary notices.

Edward Maitland spent his remaining years compiling a comprehensive two volume biography *The Life of Anna Kingsford* and publishing *Clothed with the Sun,* a complete text of her illuminations over the fourteen year period that he had known her. Some of her addresses and essays together with some letters of Maitland were later published in 1916 as *The Credo of Christendom* together with a long biographical preface, edited by Samuel Hopgood Hart.

Aleister Crowley contemptuously summed up Anna Kingsford as being a "mush head" and "black magician" - which might be regarded as a classic example of the pot calling the kettle black, and also to reveal more about himself than the victim of his jibes. Others, including some of her family, may have regarded her as an hysteric, fanatic and religious maverick – and we have to take account of her courage in the face of the rigid Victorian attitudes of the time. Even Maitland narrowly escaped being committed to an institution because his family were scandalised by his unorthodox views.

But let us allow a hard bitten contemporary journalist of her time, W.T.Stead, to have the last word upon this remarkable woman.

He wrote: "Who that ever met her can forget that marvellous embodiment of a burning flame in the form of a woman, divinely tall and not less divinely fair! ...Her movements had somewhat of the grace and majesty that we associate with the Greek gods; and as for her speech – well, I have talked to many of the men and women who have in this generation had the greatest repute as conversationalists, but I never in my life met Anna Kingsford's equal...Never was she at a loss for a word, never did she tangle her sentences, or halt for an illustration. It was almost appaling after a time. It appeared impossible for her to run dry, for you seemed to feel that copious as was her speech, it was but as a rivulet carrying off the overflow of the ocean which lay behind."

That ocean, indeed, perhaps had something of the Ain Soph, of which she would seem to have been a consummate priestess, in the light of some of the more exalted of her illuminations, such as the Immaculate Conception of the Divine Wisdom or her hymn to Pallas Athena.

9
STAR MAGIC

There are 88 constellations in the night sky by means of which astronomers divide the celestial sphere into manageable parts. There are millions of stars in the sky in many orders of brightness and magnitude but most ancient observers of the stars felt well content if they catalogued a thousand or so. The constellations are named after various figures projected into the sky by the human imagination, rather after the fashion of one of those dot-to-dot pictures to be found in children's books. Even so, it can take a considerable leap of the imagination to visualise the object referred to when one has joined up the relevant stars with imaginary lines. This suggests that in many cases at least, the image was projected onto the stars from the mind of man, rather than their inherent pattern suggesting a particular image. Therefore it can be a profitable exercise to meditate upon these patterns projected into the sky, for they form the pages of a most ancient book of mystery teaching.

Not all of the constellations are of the same antiquity, for until early modern times man had not penetrated far enough south for the southern constellations to be visible. Therefore Ptolemy, the great cataloguer of stars in third century Alexandria, who drew upon the traditions of some centuries before him, listed just forty eight. These were the twelve constellations that are associated with the signs of the Zodiac, plus thirty six others. It is these forty eight constellations that form the original book of the "starry wisdom" of the ancient world.

The zodiacal twelve form a circle of constellations through which the Sun appears to pass in the course of the year, although really it is the orbit of the Earth around the Sun that provides the circle. Most of the planets pass through these constellations too, for (with the exception of far off Pluto) the planets of the solar system are spread out in the same plane, like the surface of a dish. And although the planets are actually orbiting around the Sun, from the point of view of an observer on Earth, it is the Sun and the other planets, and our own Moon, that appear to be revolving in a circle around the Earth, within a circle in the sky marked out by the twelve zodiacal constellations.

There are actually four very bright stars, highly visible to the naked eye, that form cardinal directions in the stellar skyscape. Aldebaran in Taurus; Regulus in Leo; Antares in Scorpio just south of the constellation of Aquila, the Eagle; and Fomalhaut, the mouth of the Southern Fish, which is just below the zodiacal constellation of Aquarius, whose waters pour into it. It will be noted that these four celestial directions correspond to the traditional Holy Living Creatures, represented as the Bull, the Lion, the Eagle and the Man. This should be hint enough that there is considerable hidden teaching within these symbols, which accounts for their appearance in the Bible as part of the vision of Ezekiel, and their later allocation to the Four Apostles.

Two other important zodiacal constellations are Cancer and Capricorn. These are signs associated with the terrestrial tropic zones that are circles of latitude drawn parallel to the Equator. The Sun never appears to be directly overhead any further north than the tropic of Cancer (at the Summer Solstice) or any further south than the tropic of Capricorn (at the Winter Solstice) and is directly over the Equator at Vernal and

128

Autumnal Equinoxes – the latter being occasions for mystical celebration on account of the forces of upper and lower worlds being in equilibrium. The physical condition that gives rise to the coming and going of the seasons is the tilt of the Earth on its axis, in relation to the plane of its orbit around the Sun. If the Earth spun in a completely upright position in relation to its orbit round the Sun there would be no different seasons of the year.

What is more, each of the two constellations associated with the solstices are by tradition gates for the coming and going of human souls in and out of incarnation upon the Earth. Thus Cancer is the Gate of Birth and Capricorn the Gate of Death. The shell of the crab might be regarded as emblematic of the physical shell of the human body that is taken on at birth. Capricorn as Gate of Death, through popular misconception, has rather unjustly, if understandably, been associated with the Devil as has the goat. The goat however is a creature that can scale the mountain tops of vision with the greatest of ease – or as sea-goat (a form of sea-horse) plumb the depths of the mystic ocean.

Another zodiacal constellation of prime symbolic importance is the Virgin, and there is much that can be gleaned from meditation upon the Virgin of the Stars, whether in pagan or Christian terms, or in her role in the pantheons of classical antiquity. As depicted in illustrated star charts she bears an ear or a sheaf of corn, signifying the sowing and the harvesting of the source of the bread of life and she is a patroness of civilisation. As Astraea she also represents divine justice as ruler of a golden age, whether of paradisal past or revelationary future, and is placed next to the sign of the Scales – a relatively recent addition to the zodiac. Before their introduction, the scales she held were the claws of the Scorpion; and in her relation to Scorpio, significant of masculinity as Virgo is of femininity, there is much that is relevant to the cosmic significance of gender.

Two other related constellations are those of Sagittarius, the Archer, and Gemini the twins, their physical significance being that they point in opposite directions from our Solar system. If we were to travel in a line from the Sun to and through Sagittarius we would find ourselves at the centre of our Galaxy. If we were to travel in a line from our Sun to and through Gemini we would be travelling in exactly the opposite direction and out into cosmic space beyond the confines of our Galaxy.

Esoterically considered, Sagittarius, represented by a centaur, is a great teacher, who instructed many of the heroes, and whose bow and arrow is indicative of aspiration. In physical terms it is aiming at the very heart of our local city of stars ruled over by the Galactic Logos, a veritable King among Stars. For this reason it is appropriately assigned to the central path of the Tree of Life that leads from Yesod to Tiphareth, the point of manifest equilibrium within creation and a focus for the meeting of higher and lower consciousness.

Gemini, on the other hand, is associated with teaching on the mysteries of the spiritual immortality and the physical mortality of humanity – for the story of Castor and Pollux is of a mortal and an immortal pair of twins, indicative of the higher and the lower aspects of human consciousness.

This leaves us with two zodiacal constellations remaining – Aries, the Ram, that traditionally leads the flock and is often depicted as looking round to see that they are following him. In Christian terms it has close association with the Lamb and

Flag, the Creator and Saviour of the world, victorious in the Last Days. In classical myth the Ram was the bearer of the Golden Fleece, sought after by the questing heroes, and among the Egyptian gods Atum, the king of the gods, was depicted as ram headed.

Finally, Pisces, the Fishes, have a Christian association, for the Christian revelation came to Earth in the Piscean age. The fish was an early emblem of Christ, just as his disciples were fishers of men, and there may well be a mystical significance in the hungry multitude being fed by a miraculous abundance of fishes as well as of loaves of bread. There are also alchemical resonances, two fish, one gold and one silver in a container of water, indicating the higher and lower elements of the soul and of the universe within their aqueous element of undifferentiated consciousness. In classical myth the constellational fish are forms of Venus and Cupid, the goddess of love and her son, who is active within the world shooting his darts and transforming human hearts. In more Qabalistic terms she is Ain Soph, the great feminine matrix behind all creation, and he the cosmic Eros, a mighty Kether figure at the fount of becoming.

Very often esoteric consideration of the patterns in the stars stops with the twelve zodiacal constellations. There are, however, even in the limited catalogue of classical antiquity, a further thirty six to be considered.

One way of approaching these is to follow the track of the Milky Way through the heavens, which in physical terms is the disc of the Galaxy to which our Planet and Sun belong. It is thus arguably, in its way, as important as the circle of the zodiac. It is also, in some mythologies, a great River of Stars, and the shining of the Milky Way is, to the Amerindians, the lights of the campfires of their ancestors. In classical myth it is formed from the milk from the breast of Hera, the great Queen of the Gods, spilled after suckling the archetypal human hero, Heracles.

One way of approaching the Milky Way in magical terms is to follow it in a great circular journey, taking note of the constellations that it passes between. A useful and appropriate vehicle for such a journey is already in the stars in the form of the Argo, the magically empowered ship of the hero Jason and the Argonauts in their quest of the Golden Fleece. A ship whose building was supervised by Pallas Athene, the goddess of Wisdom, and through a fragment of oak from the shrine of Zeus, was endowed with speech and the gift of prophecy, and launched by Orpheus, whose lyre contains the secrets of the harmony of the universe.

We may envisage going aboard the Argo in company with the heroes, at the mouth of the river Eridanus, a great constellation that runs from the celestial equator southward to the great sea of the southern celestial skies. Our point of egress into deeper waters is by the constellation Gemini, which, as we have said, points in the direction of outer space, beyond the Galactic system. It will be apparent that most of the southern constellations we are about to meet are associated with the sea. The passage into the great sea is guarded by the great giant Orion of the southern skies, and his two dogs, Canis Major and Minor, the former of which contains Sirius, the brightest star in the sky, whose rising was associated with another great river, the inundation of the Nile.

Once into the open sea we find ourselves passing great monsters of the deep, Cetus the whale, and Hydra the sea serpent. Cetus is far from a benevolent basking creature, for in the myth of Andromeda, she was chained to a rock to be a sacrifice to it. Hydra has some strange ambivalent associations. A fight with this ten headed monster was one of the labours of Heracles, and it was encouraged by the goddess Hera (who rewarded the Crab which assisted it). With the ten heads reminding us of the Spheres of the Tree of Life and the Crab being associated with the Gate of physical incarnation, we may intuit certain deep mystery teachings within this strange story. In the stars, the Hydra, whose body loops above and below the surface of the ocean, like the reincarnating soul, has associated with it a Cup and a Crow – the constellations Crater and Corvus. One, we may ask, indicative of the Holy Grail or a vessel of Regeneration. The other the alchemical emblem of dissolution and the first stage of the alchemical process.

We find our direction of sail by recourse to other nearby constellations. The Centaur is reminder that our course lies toward Sagittarius, which is where the Milky Way cuts across the zodiacal circle. The Centaur also contains the closest visible star to our own Sun, Alpha Centauri, which, according to *The Cosmic Doctrine,* is said (no doubt in symbolic terms) to represent the way to the Cosmic Central Stillness. We also pass under the Southern Cross that marks the nadir of our journey as well as the southern celestial pole, and make towards Ara, the Altar, which in ancient times was synonymous with a lighthouse, and sacred to the goddess Isis. A famous example, hailed as one of the seven wonders of the world, was the great lighthouse just off Alexandria before the delta of the Nile, a fire altar burning upon a rock that must have been well known to Ptolemy, the star charter.

As we pass we may also be aware of dolphins about our ship, represented by the Dolphin constellation. Such were reputed to be the friends of mariners, and some who were shipwrecked claimed to have been taken safely to shore by them. Once ashore such castaways may also have been helped on their way home by the little horse, Equuleus, or nurtured by the wolf Lupus, who although designated as a werewolf in some legends, might better be regarded as the friendly beast who fostered Romulus and Remus, the founders of Rome.

As we approach the far side of the zodiacal wheel from which we entered the sea, we do not pass straight ahead on through Sagittarius away, and out of our solar system toward the centre of the Galaxy, but follow the Milky Way as it strikes upward parallel with the curvature of the Earth. As we do so we find that our ship has left the surface of the waters and is flying through the air. In celebration of this we might care to throw down a celebratory wreath onto the waters, which is marked by the constellation of Corona Australis, the Southern Crown, that was depicted as a wreath by the ancients.

The Argo follows the course of the Arrow, Sagitta, and as we rise upward so we find that we are accompanied by great aerial constellations – Cygnus, the Swan that as Leda was the mother of the heavenly twins, and Pegasus, the winged horse of creative inspiration. A little further off, towards which our course is set, is the great constellation of the Lyre of Orpheus, whose heavenly music provides the harmony of the spheres, and which contains the bright star Vega, which in other epochs of our earthly history marks the northern celestial pole. So it was in 18000 B.C. and so it will be again in 8000 A.D. but for the present we make towards our present polar star Polaris.

Just as the physical north pole of our Earth is located in the centre of a great frozen island so we may envisage a starry Hyperborean isle upon which are to be found the representatives of the circumpolar constellations. These form the persons of a great mythical story that is of great significance to the human condition. It consists of a King, (Cepheus), a Queen, (Cassiopeia), a Warrior Hero, (Perseus), and a Sacrificed Maiden, (Andromeda). These are archetypal figures, which have a certain resonance with the Court Cards of the Tarot. Cepheus was descended from Zeus, the king of the gods, and Io the ancient goddess who preceded Isis. He ruled over a fabulous kingdom at high altitude. Casseopia his queen was of ineffable beauty. The vulgar interpretation of their story is that because of their overweaning pride their daughter Andromeda was chained to a rock as a sacrifice to the monsters of the deep, such as Cetus, whom we have already met. There is, however, another interpretation, that is known to initiates, that sees King and Queen as holders of heavenly perfection and Andromeda as a willing sacrifice to bring a like state to the worlds beneath, with the assistance of Perseus.

The hero Perseus was divinely conceived in an underground cavern, his father manifesting as a shower of gold at his conception. He was born as a shining babe, and cast adrift upon the waters with his mother in an enclosed ark, until rescued, nurtured and taught by a Fisher King. Instructed and protected by the wisdom of Hermes and Pallas Athene he crossed the seas, passing the tests of nine goddesses, (one of whom was the Medusa), and overcoming the dragon that guarded them, brought back the golden apples from the paradisal Isles of the West, after which he was able to release Andromeda from her chains in the world below at the mercy of the monsters of the deep.

The dragon, who on Earth empowered the Delphic oracle, is to be seen coiling around the northern pole, as Draco, and in certain epochs also provides polar stars from its body. We might envisage the family of King, Queen, Hero and Maiden, sitting within a fourfold temple within a hyperborean palace like magi in a great ongoing magical rite. In the centre a great circular arena in which there is a huge millstone, that is turned by a great she-bear accompanied by her cub. That is to say, the polar constellations of Ursa Major and Ursa Minor – the former a form of the nymph Callisto who was loved by Zeus, and the latter having the current pole star, Polaris, in its tail.

In geophysical terms, it is the pole star that marks the axis of the spinning Earth as it gives us our sequences of days and nights, and has from ancient times been likened to the turning of a mill wheel or sometimes as a whirlpool – at any rate a great swirling vortex of cosmic force that turns the Earth and gives the vista of the ever turning sphere of the heavens.

The Andromeda/Perseus myth is one that will repay considerable meditation, and it was not for nothing that those who designed the Golden Dawn version of the Tarot cards elected to name one card, the Lovers, after this mythological cycle. It also has considerable thought provoking offshoots, concerning for example the Medusa, (whose head in stellar terms is the variable star Algol in the belt of Perseus), who originally was a beautiful goddess, associated with the mare, but who took on her frightful form after making love in a temple of wisdom. Even so, one interpretation of her reputation for turning men to stone may have been not her ugliness but her supernal beauty, so ravishing, that no-one could look upon her and live. When she was overcome by Perseus it was her blood dropping into the sea that gave birth to the creature of poetic inspiration, the winged horse Pegasus, closely associated with the nine muses of the sun god Apollo.

We should not neglect however, a quadrivium of heroes who look on at this circumpolar pageant, and in certain respects are associated with it —Auriga, the charioteer; Bootes, the bear herd. Heracles of the twelve great labours; Ophiuchus, the serpent bearer. Auriga is closely associated with the Sun for in some versions of his myth it is he who drives the solar chariot through the skies. Bootes is he who oversees the turning of the wheel of the heavens in his function as driver of the bears, although he is sometimes known as the Ploughman when the Little Bear is referred to as the Plough. Heracles is a great human figure, whose many adventures might be said to reflect the long history of the human race, although some see him as a sun hero, passing through the twelve signs of the zodiac as his twelve labours. Perhaps greatest of all is Ophiuchus, the serpent bearer, closely associated with the constellation Serpens. This is the serpent of wisdom carried by great magi such as Moses and Aaron, or the serpent of healing carried by Asclepios, the great patron of medicine.

We have now accounted in one way or another for most of Ptolemy's fortyeight constellations and many may feel that this is quite enough to be going on with as a curriculum for the starry mysteries. However, as navigation and exploration improved in early modern times, so did vistas of the southern skies open up that had never been seen before. This accounts for the great majority of forty or so remaining constellations that make up to the modern total of eighty eight.

The mapping of new constellations reflects the concerns of observers of the times, and they came in three broad phases.

Twelve were introduced as a result of the southern voyages of the Dutchmen Pieter Keyser and Frederick de Houtman encouraged by the theologian and cartographer Petrus Plancius, and which were incorporated into Johann Bayer's star atlas of 1603.

These were for the most part quite exotic creatures. Apus, the Bird of Paradise; the Chameleon; Dorado, the Goldfish; Grus, the Crane; Hydrus, a lesser sea monster; Indus, the Indian; Musca the Fly,; Pavo, the Peacock; Phoenix, the regenerating fire bird; Tucana the Toucan; Volans, the Flying Fish; together with a Southern Triangle to match one that is found in the northern skies.

This was an interesting period when science had not yet taken on an exclusively materialist trend, and new human knowledge could have an esoteric dimension too. Thus it can be instructive to let the imagination run free to allow associations to rise that may make these constellations vehicles for magical interpretation. Most obvious is the Phoenix, with its regenerative powers and immortality; and another immortal creature, the Bird of Paradise – which has its equivalent in the oriental Garuda bird. The Peacock has ever been associated with the goddess Hera, whilst admirers of Robert Graves will be aware of the esoteric aspects of the Crane, whose close relation the Stork is also associated with new birth. The Fly tends to have rather unfortunate associations but it was first entitled the Bee, and perhaps a Fire-fly or a Humming Bird might be nearer the original conception. Both the Chameleon and the Goldfish have alchemical associations, and the Flying Fish is a creature that is at home in Air and Water, just as the Phoenix is with Air and Fire. A Southern Triangle to complement the one in the northern sky gives us the elements of the Six-Rayed Star which is the emblem of the conjoining of higher and lower consciousness in the attained initiate.

A Polish astronomer, Johannes Hevelius endeavoured to fill up gaps in the northern sky in a star atlas of 1690. He added eleven but only seven have been generally accepted. These are Canes Venatici, the Hunting Dogs; Lacerta, the Lizard; Leo Minor, the little Lion; Lynx; Scutum, the Shield; Sextans, the Sextant; and Vulpecula, the Fox.

The Hunting Dogs, were a part of the Great Bear, and Hevelius assigned them to the care of Bootes as a means of keeping the Bears in order. Its brightest star has become associated with King Charles I, the martyr king, as Cor Caroli, the Heart of Charles. However, some also associated it with his son, Charles II, on the grounds that it shone particularly brightly at the Restoration at the end of May 1660.

The Lizard was placed between Cygnus and Andromeda and was alternatively named Stellio, the Starry Newt, although this never caught on, despite it being quite an evocative image, somewhat reminiscent of a sparky salamander. Leo Minor, was a cub introduced to accompany the major constellation Leo, just to the north of it.

The Lynx was placed in a large area of sky without bright stars between the Great Bear and Auriga, and because it is so difficult to see with the naked eye Hevelius is thought to have named it after Lynceus, one of the Argonauts who had the sharpest eyesight in the world, including the ability to see underground. This has obvious esoteric ramifications, although the Lynx itself might also be invoked as one of the creatures sacred to Venus.

The Shield, close to the Milky Way near Sagittarius and Aquila, was originally called Sobiesci's Shield, in honour of a Polish nobleman who helped Hevelius after his observatory burnt to the ground. Sextans, another very faint constellation just south of Leo, celebrates the Sextant which Hevelius used to make his star observations. He is considered something of a crank nowadays because he refused to use a telescope, even though they were by then widely available. There are good esoteric reasons for this however, as has been elaborated by Owen Barfield, one of the most intelligent interpreters of the occultist Rudolf Steiner – insofar that what is visible to the naked eye is of greater significance than anything that can only be observed through the eye-piece of an optical instrument. This argument carries greater force nowadays in the era of radio-astronomy, where star images of far distant skies are in fact artificial reconstructions of mathematical data rather than direct observation on a human scale. (Refer to Barfield's *Saving the Appearances* for more eludication of this.)

Vulpeculla, the Fox was originally conceived as the Fox and Goose by Helvelius and although astronomers have abandoned the latter creature it is questionable why either were needed; they appear in a virtually blank area of sky near Cygnus.

The final major addition to the company of constellations was the mapping of the southern skies by the French astronomer Lacaille, who set up an observatory at Table Mountain in South Africa and in 1754 produced a map with fourteen new southern hemisphere constellations.

His Table Mountain site was honoured by Mensa, the Table, and his other constellations reflect the burgeoning of the scientific method at this dawn of the modern age. Thus we have Antlia, Caelum, Circinus, Fornax Chemica, Horologium,

Microscopium, Norma, Octans, Pictor, Pyxis, Reticulum, Sculptor and Telescopium, signifying respectively the Air Pump, the Graving Tool, the Pair of Compasses, the Chemical Furnace, the Pendulum Clock, the Microscope, the Level, the Octant, the Painter's Easel, the Mariner's Compass, the Net, the Sculptor's Workshop and the Telescope.

This is not to say that there is no esoteric mileage in all of this. The Air Pump, which gave the possibility of a vacuum, was an almost magical device in the early days; we take the presence of the air for granted nowadays but Charles II, who founded the Royal Society, could not understand how these men of science could be so scatterbrained as to try to measure something so patently non-existent as air. Some figures have masonic resonances, others alchemical, navigational or artistic whilst the Net is a symbol of very ancient and wide esoteric potential, whilst the sculptor's workshop may conjure speculations about the significance of Pygmalion, who fell in love with his own creation.

There remains but to mention of one or two maverick constellations that have not appeared so far. A most unlikely one is Camelopardalis, the Giraffe, which was placed between Cassiopeia and Ursa Major by Petrus Plancius in 1613, apparently in some confusion with the camel that took Rebecca to Canaan to be married to Isaac. This is an example of a number of attempts of various individuals to place their own conceptions into the sky, although most of them did not gain popular acceptance. This includes an attempt to rename the constellations after Biblical characters but the stars remain staunchly independent of such ecclesiastical ambitions.

Perhaps the most evocative of latter day constellations is a contribution of Tycho Brahe, a Danish nobleman of legendary personal characteristics, who constructed a star castle, the Uraniborg, upon an island called Hvena, or Venusia, not far from Hamlet's Elsinore that lies in the channel between Denmark and Sweden. He is celebrated in part of an epic poetic sequence by the once highly popular poet Alfred Noyes, in *Watchers of the Stars,* in which he is depicted in a very magical four-fold set-up. Married to a peasant girl, Katrina, and having a hunchback dwarf with prophetic powers, called Jeppe, as personal servant, he himself wore a gold mask, to hide a duelling scar, and with armour and a long cloak had an aspect not entirely divorced from the legendary Odin. The flag that flew over his star castle bore the emblem of the winged horse Pegasus. His contribution to astronomy was significant. He compiled a catalogue of a thousand stars, correcting errors in the ancient star charts, using great wooden instruments of his own invention. His principal assistant was Johannes Kepler, a mathematician of strong neo-platonic leanings, who unsuccessfully tried to relate the orbits of the planets with the Platonic solids, but in the end worked out the laws of planetary orbital motion. Both later ended up in that most alchemical of cities, Prague, the capital of Bohemia.

Tycho's contribution to the list of constellations was Berenice's Hair, celebrating the moving story of an Egyptian queen who sacrificed her crowning glory upon the altar of the love goddess in thanksgiving for bringing her husband back safely from the wars. The constellation was known to the ancient Greeks but was considered by them to form part of Leo. Tycho felt it deserved independent status, and since his day it has also been recognised as indicating the direction of the Galactic Pole, the axis about which the Milky Way spins.

The ancient Greek Eratosthenes considered it to be the hair of Ariadne, (she who guided Theseus through the labyrinth), and associated it with another beautiful northern constellation Corona Borealis, the Northern Crown, whose brightest star is Gemma, the jewel. It is also known as Ariadne's Crown, which was worn by her when she married Dionysus, who flung it into the skies to prove to her/his status as a god.

This has been of necessity rather a rapid gallop through the star fields, but there are a number of well illustrated astronomical books about these days, and letting the imagination roam through them can provide a practical mode of instruction that can be as rewarding as any more overtly esoteric text. Better still, go out and observe the stars yourself. They are your link to the cosmos. But remember that we owe our first loyalty to that great star in whose ambience we live and move and have our being, the Day Star, the Sun. And as C.S.Lewis pointed out in his theologically inspired science fiction trilogy, we do not need to try to pass out into space, as inhabitants of the Earth we are already in it!

THE ESOTERIC STUDIES OF
THE SOCIETY OF THE INNERLIGHT

DION FORTUNE, founder of The Society of the Inner Light, is recognised as one of the most luminous and significant figures of 20th Century esoteric thought. A brilliant writer, pioneer psychologist and powerful psychic, she dedicated her life to the revival of the Mystery Tradition of the West and she left behind her a solidly established knowledge of many systems, ancient and modern.

This special edition brings together two immensely valuable classic books which make the complex foundations of psychic development accessible to all readers.

ESOTERIC ORDERS AND THEIR WORK examines how occultists have jealously restricted admission to their secret societies and schools and shrouded their practices in mystery. Dion Fortune here uncovers the workings of these secret organisations and describes their operations in detail.

THE TRAINING AND WORK OF AN INITIATE shows how, from their ancient roots, the Western Esoteric Systems have an unbroken tradition of European initiation that has been handed down from adept to neophyte. This book indicates the broad outlines and underlying principles of these systems in order to illuminate an obscure and greatly misunderstood aspect of the Path.

ISBN 0 - 85030 - 664 - 7

APPLIED MAGIC is a selection of Dion Fortune's writings on the practical applications of magical and occult techniques. Written from the point of view of a gifted psychic, they provide invaluable and suggestive pointers to anyone intent on increasing their inner awareness.

ASPECTS OF OCCULTISM looks at nine specific aspects of the Western Mystery Tradition, including God and the Gods, Sacred Centres, The Astral Plane, The Worship of Isis, Teachings Concerning the Aura, and the Pitfalls of Spiritual Healing

ISBN 0 - 85030 - 665 - 5

THE ABBEY PAPERS
By Gareth Knight

The Abbey Papers, which comprise this book, came to Gareth Knight over a period of ninety days, apparently stimulated by some editorial work he had been doing upon the War Letters of Dion Fortune, subsequently published as Dion Fortune's Magical Battle of Britain.

He had not particularly sought to set up as a channel of communication in this way but the initiative seemed to come from within, nagging away at him compulsively, much as some poets are pressured by their muse, until he sat down and did something about it – if only to prove that all was nonsense or of no great consequence. To his surprise it all started to flow quite readily and the fact that it now appears in print means that at least he and the publishers feel that there is something within it all that is worth sharing.

ISBN 1 899585 80 X

DION FORTUNE AND THE THREE FOLD WAY

The chapters in this book consist of articles that appeared in the Inner Light Journal, house journal of the Society of the Inner Light, between Spring 1997 and December 2001. They have as a common theme, aspects of the life and work of Dion Fortune, founder of the Society.

Dion Fortune and the British Mysteries was first given as a talk on 15th September 2001 to the Wildwood Conference, Conway Hall, London, organised by Atlantis Bookshop.

ISBN 1 899585 70 2

THE MAGIC RAILWAY
By David Williams

Fairy story or esoteric pathworking - following a long tradition!

The lives of the Selby children are threatened with disruption as their Media World parents part. They are consigned to the care of the fearsome Gerda in Notting Hill. The previous owner has mysteriously vanished. Mr Pretorius it seems was a great traveller on an extra dimensional magical railway from Nothing Hill Gate. Together they follow in his tracks and the youngest, Rosy, finds herself the centre focus for a life and death struggle involving the Grail and the restoration of order and balance to the world.

ISBN 1 899585 61 3

GRANNY'S PACK OF CARDS
By Gareth Knight

There is much more to the Tarot than a curious game as Rebecca and Richard discover. Illustrated. Publication 2003

A children's fantasy story by Gareth Knight. Richard and Rebecca meet the Joker of their granny's magic pack of cards and, assisted by his dog, meet many of his friends on a hair raising cycle of adventures that takes them to many strange worlds such as the Mountains of the Stars beyond the Gates of Time and thence to the Wondrous Island at the Heart of the Rainbow.

Any correspondence with the figures they meet and the pictures in the Tarot pack are entirely coincidental – but we all know what coincidences are – and they receive much fascinating instruction on this and that by characters as diverse as the Star Maiden and the Great Emperor, having evaded such dangers as the DarkTower and the Desert Reapers. All ends happily with their triumphant return to Myrtle Cottage having made some acquaintance with their True Names and Essential Goodnesses.

ISBN 1 899585 85 0

DION FORTUNE TAROT CARDS

Strangely the Society of the Inner Light did not produce a Tarot pack although its symbolism is a feature of her classic MYSTICAL QABBALAH.

Now at last is a version of the Tarot in line with Dion Fortune's understanding and that of the Order of the Golden Dawn. All the suits of the Lesser Arcana have been illustrated with images reflecting their symbolism from classical times to the present day. The explanatory booklet also gives guidance on Tarot pathworkings, which are valuable psycho/spiritual exercises and a very positive use of the Kabbalistic Tree of Life.

ISBN 1 899585 75 3

THE DEMON LOVER

Young and innocent Veronica is taken on as Mr. Lucas' secretary though he has other plans for her... Without fully realising just what is going on Veronica finds herself involved in the work of a mysterious sinister male-only magical Lodge. In spite of Lucas' ruthless exploitation she falls in love with him and becomes an accessory in his occult workings.

To try to protect her from the wrath of the Lodge because of her unlooked for and unwanted attraction, Alec Lucas is immersed deeper and deeper into the darkness of the Underworld, ever struggling to free himself from many hells.

This was Dion Fortune's first novel, based on real characters and experiences. It offers many insights not only into the inner nature of the Mysteries and the dangers of Black Magic but also defines aspects of the sacred nature of love.

When it was published the Times Literary Supplement considered it to be 'exceedingly well-written', and it has stood the test of time.

ISBN 1 899585 30 3

THE ESOTERIC PHILOSOPHY OF LOVE AND MARRIAGE

Dion Fortune's basic esoteric textbook on the psychology of love and relationships give a simple explanation of the universal factors governing interaction between masculine and feminine from the 'lowest' to the 'highest' level of the Seven Planes.

This sensitive and authoritative account, written by a distinguished woman who combined uncanny intuition with "hands on" psychological experience clearly states the principles of polarity underlying all relationships between men and women with insight and sensitivity.

These principles remain as true today as when this classic guide was first published, at the time it was fully realised that a formal marriage contract or ceremony would in no way neutralise or diminish the tensions of sexual incompatibility caused by temperamental differences, conflicting goals or destinies.

Sex is a function, not an ideal and there are other factors producing harmony or otherwise. The feminine is 'positive' on the Spiritual Plane and that of the Emotions. While the masculine tends to be more 'positive' on the Mental and Physical planes. In a proper union, these aspects are harmoniously complementary so the relationship remains in balance. Where these aspects are unrecognised and are denied free expression, disharmony can often result. Needless to say the physical expression through sex will also suffer, since attitudes derived from the 'higher' levels control or inhibit the 'lower' physical aspect.

THE ESOTERIC PHILOSOPHY OF LOVE AND MARRIAGE also includes Dion Fortune's teaching on some of the esoteric principles behind abstinence and asceticism, contraception and abortion.

ISBN 1 899585 25 7

THE COSMIC DOCTRINE

Seventy two years ago a remarkable event took place beginning at the Vernal Equinox in Glastonbury. For very nearly a year Dion Fortune received communications from the Inner Planes concerning the Creation of the Universe, which later became a classic.

THE COSMIC DOCTRINE remained a closely guarded secret until 1949 when a closely edited version was privately printed since Dion Fortune's successor considered the original "a most dangerous book".

It is now available for the first time in its entirety in the original text in this definitive edition.

This full text examines the no man's land where Science and Magic interact. The Cosmology of the "Big Bang" and Chaos Theory running parallel to the evolutionary process. Each Human Spirit volunteering to learn the lessons and acquire the experience going hand in hand with the physical Universe.

But a cryptic warning accompanies these clearly outlined concepts; this book is designed to train the mind rather than inform it. In other words it is intended to induce a particular attitude both to the inner and outer world. Most must realise, words can hardly describe the immensity of the Cosmic creative process and the manifold complexity of our planetary and atomic systems under the jurisdiction of the Solar Logos.

THE COSMIC DOCTRINE further illustrates the true nature of Good and Evil which man generally views from his own highly subjective and very personal perspective. There are further insights into the interaction of positive and negative polarity within the universal scheme of things.

Besides the Creation of the Universe and the evolution of Mankind the COSMIC DOCTRINE has much to teach about Natural Law, the evolution of Consciousness and the Nature of Mind.

Illustrated with diagrams by one of Dion Fortune's closest collaborators.

ISBN 1 899585 0 52

GLASTONBURY, AVALON OF THE HEART

Dion Fortune first visited Glastonbury while Bligh Bond was still uncovering its past with his amazing psychic investigations into the Abbey ruins. It was at Glastonbury also that she received her first major and dramatic Inner Plane contact in Chalice Orchard close to Chalice Well.

Later she acquired the plot of the land and established a retreat, where it had all happened, under the shadow of the Tor.

AVALON OF THE HEART is her personal account of the love affair with Glastonbury that drew her back repeatedly across the years.

Her description remains one of the most evocative and poignant accounts of this wild yet holy place; a power centre polarising with distant Jerusalem and linking and harmonising the Christian way with the primaeval and pagan past.

She includes as a background time honoured legends of Joseph of Arimathea, the Grail and Arthur the King with special insights since she, more than any other, re-established these long overlooked historic matters of the Isles of Britain with special authority.

AVALON OF THE HEART is besides, both lyrical and poetic, recapturing the timelessly inspiring mood of Glastonbury, as she knew and loved it.

To pilgrims of the Aquarian Age her account is a precious reminder of Britain's heritage and its deep roots in the past. Not only that, but a gateway to the future.

With black and white illustrations by Peter Arthy.

ISBN 1 899585 20 6

MACHINERY OF THE MIND

"One of the shortest and clearest of the many popular books on modern psychology which have been published."

When she was barely twenty Dion Fortune was working in London just before the 1914-18 War as a lay analyst and so obtained first hand practical insights into that aspects of the human condition. Her subsequent esoteric work placed a heavy emphasis on the unwisdom of embarking on the Mysteries without thorough inner preparation. In a perfect world this would mean that candidates for initiation would present themselves with a clean bill of psychological health.

machinery of the mind was considered sufficiently important to form part of the standard background reading for the Study Course offered by the Society of the Inner Light that Dion Fortune founded.

ISBN 1 899585 00 1

THE MYSTICAL QABALAH

Dion Fortune's THE MYSTICAL QABALAH remains a classic in its clarity, linking the broad elements of Jewish traditional thought - probably going back to the Babylonian Captivity and beyond - with both eastern and western philosophy and later Christian insights.

Dion Fortune was one of the first Adepts to bring this 'secret tradition' to a wider audience. Some before her often only added to the overall mystery by elaborating on obscurity, but her account is simple, clear and comprehensive.

The Qabalah could be described as a confidential Judaic explanation of the paradox of 'the Many and the One' - the complexity and diversity within a monotheistic unity. Whereas the Old Testament outlines the social and psychological development of a tightly knit 'chosen group' culture, the supplementary Qabalah provides a detailed plan of the infrastructure behind the creative evolutionary process.

A major limitation of the Authorised English Version of the bible is the translation of the many Hebrew God-names by the single name "God". THE MYSTICAL QABALAH devotes a chapter to each of the ten schematic 'God-names', the qualities or 'Sephiroth', which focus the principle archetypes behind evolving human activity: the Spiritual Source; the principles of Force and Form; Love and Justice; the Integrative principle or the Christ Force; Aesthetics and Logic; the dynamics of the Psyche and finally, the Manifestation of life in earth in a physical body.

THE MYSTICAL QABALAH works in a profoundly psychological way. Its lessons for the individual are invaluable and this book is a must for all who feel drawn to getting to know themselves better so that their inner world and their outer world may be at one.

ISBN 1 899585 35 4

PSYCHIC SELF-DEFENCE

When she was twenty, Dion Fortune found herself the subject of a particularly powerful form of psychic attack, which ultimately led to a nervous breakdown. With the benefit of hindsight, and her experience as a practising occultist and natural psychic, she wrote Psychic Self Defence, a detailed   instruction manual for protection against paranormal malevolence.

Within these pages are amazing revelations concerning the practices of Black Lodges, the risks involved in ceremonial magic, the pathology of non-human contacts, the nature of hauntings and the reality behind the ancient legends of the vampire. In addition, the book explores the elusive psychic elements in mental illness and, more importantly, details the methods, the motives, and the physical aspects of psychic attack - and how to overcome them.

Dion Fortune was born Violet Mary Frith in LLandudno, 1880. A brilliant writer and pioneer psychologist, she became increasingly interested in her own psychism and the study of magic. She went on to become a powerful medium, mystic and magician and devoted her life to her role as priestess of Isis and founder of the Society of the Inner Light, until her death from leukaemia in 1946.

ISBN 1 899585 40 0

MOON MAGIC

BEING THE MEMOIRS OF A MISTRESS OF THAT ART

The Sequel to The Sea Priestess

The manuscript of this novel was found among the author's papers and tells the return of Morgan Le Fay, the bewitching, ageless heroine first met with in The Sea Priestess. This fiction classic is last in the series planned by Dion Fortune and which was designed to impart much of the teaching of the Western Esoteric Tradition.

The story centres round an enchanting love affair that will appeal both to those searching below the surface for the principles and tenets behind the Western Esoteric Tradition as well as to the connoisseur of good fiction. Both will be fascinated by this modern tale of Magic and Mystery, with the Old Gods as Archetypes and demonstrating their power to affect us in the world today.

For a mysterious cloaked figure continually haunts the dreams of Dr.Robert Malcolm, a caring, successful yet unfulfilled medical practitioner: The image grips his imagination until it becomes close to a reality, ever moving softly ahead of him at dusk through the damp London streets, and mirroring the reflection of his nightly dreamscape.

...Until late one fateful evening, the substance of his dreams enters his surgery, unheralded yet in person... the unforgettable and eternally attractive Morgan Le Fay.

Then as Priestess of Isis she gradually returns him to the Natural World he has for so long abandoned. Taking on the painstaking task of renewing his soul and masculine power within the confines of her secret magical temple.

As time goes on, the chemistry between them stabilises into a clearly defined polarity and Dr. Malcolm is transformed in the process.

MOON MAGIC is a classic account and exploration of the interplay between masculine and feminine, anima and animus and a searching study of human and superhuman relationship.

ISBN 1 899585 15 X

THROUGH THE GATES OF DEATH

The text explains the stages in the natural process of dying that every departing soul passes though from this world to the next. The correct attitude being that death is simply birth into a new form of life and therefore to be regarded as a joyful and positive event.

Dion Fortune further sets out the requisite states of mind as well as the necessary actions by which those closest to the deceased can speed and smooth their passing and which should accompany the natural progression of death, laying out, burial and mourning.

This handbook has proved to be an invaluable aid and comfort to all confronted with bereavement, whatever their situation; whether seeking to do what is best for a departed loved one or to widen their own perception to bridge the mysteries between Life and Death.

ISBN 1 899585 10 9

THE GOAT FOOT GOD

Desperate and wretched after his wife's death at the hands of her lover, Hugh Paston turns to the Ancient Mysteries in search of Pan to re-establish and confirm his own manhood. With another seeker, Paston acquires an old monastery intending to convert it to a temple of Pan. The building is troubled by the spirit of a fifteenth century prior, walled up for his heretically pagan beliefs, who also searched for the goat-foot God. This entity plans to take over Paston's body to pursue his unremitting quest and it is left to Mona, Paston's partner's niece to help solve the problem of human love in this case, when in reality man and woman become representatives of the God and the Goddess.

'Shoots with remarkable success at a most ambitious target.' – The Guardian.

ISBN 1 899585 06 0

THE MAGICAL BATTLE OF BRITAIN

Immediately following Germany's invasion of Poland, which resulted in Britain's declaration of war, Dion Fortune, the founder of Britain's foremost magical order - The Society of The Inner Light - initiated a magical programme designed to thwart the expansionist intentions of the Third Reich, and thus the invasion of Britain.

Now, fifty years on, those instruction papers have been released from the archives of her school. Accompanied by a commentary from Gareth Knight, himself a student of Dion Fortune's fraternity, these teachings offer the reader an astonishing insight into the workings of a genuine esoteric school and their - until now - hidden yet significant contribution to the Nation's war effort.

ISBN 1 - 899585 - 00 - 1

THE SECRETS OF DR TAVERNER

Based on real people, this collection of short stories, presents Dion Fortune's teacher (said to be Dr Moriarty) with herself cast in the role of his assistant, Rhodes. Taverner uses his abilities to cure the severely mentally disturbed by esoteric techniques. By technical work on the inner planes he frees his patients from frustration, misery and worse. Rhodes, though just a learner, becomes more and more engrossed in the work until the day she overreaches herself, just like the Sorcerer's Apprentice; only just escaping terror-drenched disaster.

Each story highlights a psycho-esoteric aspect; vampirism, astral journeying, karmic repercussions, demonic interference; and this edition includes a previously unpublished story.

ISBN 1 899585 02 8

THE SEA PRIESTESS

In Dion Fortune's own words; "This book stands on its own feet as a literary Melchizedek."

It is a book with an undercurrent; upon the surface a romance; underneath a thesis upon a theme; "All women are Isis and Isis is all women."

Further, it is an experiment in prose rhythms which beat upon the subconscious mind in the same way as the Eastern Mantra, which, because they are archaic, speak to the archaic level of the mind whence dreams arise.

Dion Fortune considered with some reason, that the psychological state of modern civilisation was hardly much of an improvement on the sanitation of a mediaeval walled city. So she dedicated this work to the great goddess Cloacina, whose function it was to cleanse the drains of the Ancient Rome.

Wilfred Maxwell, a 'wimp' by any standards, learns to assert himself, his creativity and full masculinity under the tutelage of the mysterious Vivien Le Fay Morgan. His asthmatic condition has induced a certain psychism and he has a dream vision at the full moon of his patroness as the High Priestess of the Ancient Moon cult who has returned to calm and control the sea by the house he is now embellishing.

ISBN 1 899585 50 8

THE WINGED BULL: A ROMANCE OF MODERN MAGIC

The message of the book concerns the spiritualising of sex. But not the spiritualising of sex by sublimating it onto other planes than the spiritual, but the spiritualising of sex by realising its profound spiritual significance and far-reaching psychological values.

The man whom Ursula Brangwyn loves becomes involved in Black Magic and drags her after him. Her brother, a student of strange arts, knows that the only way he can rescue her is to make her transfer her affections to someone else. He chooses his man and sets to work on his difficult task, making use of certain aspects of the sex relationship that are the carefully guarded secrets of the initiates. The story shows the deliberate building of a curious magnetic rapport between two people who do not attract each other. A highly strung, highly cultured sophisticated girl and an unemployed ex-officer, hard bitten and disillusioned.

ISBN 1 899585 45 1

THE SOCIETY OF THE INNER LIGHT

The Society of the Inner Light is a Society for the study of Metaphysical Religion, Mysticism, and Esoteric Psychology. Their development of their practice.

Its aims are Christian and its methods are Western.

Students can take the Correspondence Course for training in Esoteric Science and developing the daily discipline which can lead to Initiation. Application forms and a copy of the Society's WORK AND AIMS are available from;

The Secretariat
The Society of the Inner Light
38 Steele's Road
London NW3 4RG
England

email - sil@innerlight.org.uk